Progressive Recovery
through the Twelve Steps

Emotionally Sober for Life

૭ð·

Ronald Chapman

Addiction Progresses . . . So Must Recovery

Seeing True Press
PO Box 29629 | Atlanta, GA 30359
www.SeeingTrue.com

All profits will be used to develop free content for
those in recovery at ProgressiveRecovery.org

BOOK DESIGN: Lila Romero

FIRST EDITION
Paperback ISBN: 978-0-578-43902-0
E-book ISBN: 978-0-578-43355-4

Recovery is a launching pad, not a safe haven.
—RONALD CHAPMAN

Table of Contents

Table of Contents

Introduction—My Story

In 1985, my life began to unravel. I had just been promoted with a Fortune 100 company. My wife and I were in route to a new work location when out of the blue she announced she no longer loved me and was leaving. Within months she departed to pursue a life on her own, and I discovered I was alcoholic and that I had serious health problems. The result was moderately severe depression. These experiences produced a bottom in my life, and I was struck sober. Over the next two years, everything changed, including the loss of my career. Fortunately, the Twelve Steps and the rooms of recovery bore much fruit. Ever so slowly the life of a sober, spiritual man took hold.

At five years in sobriety I married again. I was sure I was on solid ground after so much recovery, step-work and therapy. Later I was dumbfounded at how inept I was in the marriage. The difficulties I ran into pushed me deeply into learning about unconditional love with the help of my sponsor and spiritual advisor as well as my therapist. Then much to my surprise, a divorce from my second wife forced me to explore a broken heart, and heal while still maintaining unconditional love for my ex-wife.

On the day I celebrated my tenth year in recovery from alcoholism, I suddenly became aware I knew nothing about what it is to be happy, joyous and free. The resulting dive into the Twelve Steps with a new and experienced spiritual mentor produced still greater growth and development than I even imagined was possible. For the first time I came to see patterns within me that had dogged my steps all the way back to childhood.

At 17 years sober and after another failed relationship, I checked myself into an inpatient treatment center for a week of intensive love addiction and codependency intervention. I had a breakthrough there. For the first time I overcame a deep fear of my own inadequacy. That profound psychic change was transformative like nothing else that had come before it. It brought a dramatic increase in awareness and understanding of myself and my challenges, an awareness that was previously unavailable to me. More importantly, I saw that long before I became addicted to substances I had been addicted to the pursuit of nurturance and love.

One would think I had now arrived. Yet the several years leading up to my 25th anniversary in recovery comprised a period I now call my time in the wilderness. If that sounds painful, it was. The result is that today I have come to know a degree of emotional sobriety that is amazing to me. I do not mean that I somehow manage my emotions today, which are and remain forever unmanageable. Rather, as the consequence of what I know today to be the results of the Twelve Steps practiced at depth over time, many of my dependencies have simply lost their power.

Today when I tell my story, I speak most often of a deep

need for increasing spiritual exploration, not to glorify me, but to increase the degrees of freedom from myself. The result is to further distance myself from alcoholism, and to find greater and greater well-being.

In the end, it is my experience, strength and hope that the purpose of the Twelve Steps, practiced progressively, is to restore us to wholeness. That restoration happens in stage after stage after stage, seemingly without end. The possibilities and potential are only limited by our ability to practice the work of spiritual recovery time after time with increasing depth.

More than 30 years ago a spiritual advisor captured my attention with a profound observation. "Ron," he said with deadly earnestness, "Yesterday's sobriety is insufficient for today."

I remember that moment because of the truth I heard in his remark. Today my experience would tell me to say it slightly differently: A progressive addiction requires a progressive recovery. But what is meant by Progressive Recovery?

That's what this book is intended to address. Not to replace a solid Twelve Step program of recovery, but to facilitate still more progress.

Much of my time is now spent providing workshops and mentoring to promote recovery, letting go and healing. I am an Internationally Accredited Speaker through Toastmasters International, and own two consulting companies through which I lead workshops, coach and speak far beyond the rooms of recovery. The approaches I use are often based on the principles within the Twelve Steps, and sometimes are overtly spirituality-based, or designed using therapeutic techniques learned when I acquired a Master's in Social Welfare. In 2012, my writing career went to another level with the publication of my third book, *A Killer's Grace*, a novel that explores inherent innocence and the path to redemption. The lead character in that story is in recovery, and is loosely based on my life in recovery. These achievements add to three other books, two audio sets and a substantial online presence for Progressive Recovery (www.ProgressiveRecovery.org) and psycho-spiritual transformation (www.SeeingTrue.com). All this is the fruit of the spiritual recovery that began with the need to get sober.

Here is what I know to be true today:

Recovery is a launching pad, not a safe haven.

Those are the words adapted from the wisdom of a few of my sober elders. Today they play out as the realization of my potential as a human being in spiritual recovery. The whole of my story is simply stunning. I say that with great humility and gratitude. In the dedication to my first book, I said it simply. There are no self-made men or women. I am the product of the support, guidance and love of many others on a path of ever-deepening spirituality, and the principles of the Twelve Steps reflected in Progressive Recovery.

This is our shared future: a progressive realization of physical and emotional sobriety. With this comes a life that, while completely unpredictable, we could never even imagine.

Don't stop wherever you may find yourself. At worst, the progressive nature of addiction and life will catch you from behind. At best, there are no limits to our possibilities.

RONALD CHAPMAN, JANUARY 2019

An Affirmation of Experience, Strength and Hope

We are women and men in recovery who have been involved in applying these ideas together as individuals and in study groups. We want to have our say about Progressive Recovery and its supplemental approach to twelve-step recovery.

We have long-term recovery, and our experience crosses all the Twelve Step programs though most of us are affiliated with Alcoholics Anonymous first and foremost. In our perspective, Progressive Recovery is an idea whose time is upon us. We believe we are only the beginning of a wave of a deepening practice of twelve-step recovery. The more structured and concrete the approaches become, the more they will be utilized because of their value.

Even before we have completed our first sessions as small groups, we have more friends who are interested in getting into the next round.

We think the reason is simple.

Many of us have worked very good programs of recovery that included the Twelve Steps, sponsorship, meetings, service, and the like. And many of us have also had a great deal of therapeutic support. Still, just as Ron describes in his opening story, we find we get stuck. Something needs our attention, something that has not been addressed or resolved. While we believe in the steps and the program of recovery, we needed that extra something.

When we were exposed to Progressive Recovery, and saw that it used a familiar foundation and language, we were willing to give it a try. Then when it made sense and began to produce results, we were convinced. It has clearly opened up possibilities we simply were unable to attain previously.

Much of this book is based on our experience and our recommendations to Ron. While he created much of the approach out of necessity, we are pleased to have been involved with his learning and to have provided feedback. We believe in it and recommend it. We also recommend you trust what Ron has to teach. There's a great deal here to learn, and we find him to be entirely trustworthy to carry the message.

Andy D.	Eric R.	Maggie N.
Amy H.	Eve T.	Michelle P.
Caroline H.	Joey K.	Nance W.
Chris A.	Karen M.	Steven W.
Debbie M.	Linda J.	Susan R.

The Story of Emotional Sobriety

In 1958 the *AA Grapevine* published *The Next Frontier: Emotional Sobriety* by Alcoholics Anonymous co-founder Bill Wilson. At that time, with more than 20 years in sobriety and no small amount of remarkable personal and spiritual growth, Bill continued to suffer from debilitating depression. It was a matter with which he wrestled in any number of ways, coming over and over again to uncovering the root causes of his difficulties.

It was in this amazing piece that he first articulated the notion of emotional sobriety, that somehow there must be a way to escape the debilitating cycle of great emotional upheavals.

> I kept asking myself, "Why can't the Twelve Steps work to release depression?" By the hour, I stared at the St. Francis Prayer ... "It's better to comfort than to be the comforted." Here was the formula, all right. But why didn't it work?
>
> Suddenly I realized what the matter was. My basic flaw had always been dependence—almost absolute dependence—on people or circumstances to supply

me with prestige, security, and the like. Failing to get these things according to my perfectionist dreams and specifications, I had fought for them. And when defeat came, so did my depression...

Because I had over the years undergone a little spiritual development, the absolute quality of these frightful dependencies had never before been so starkly revealed. Reinforced by what Grace I could secure in prayer, I found I had to exert every ounce of will and action to cut off these faulty emotional dependencies upon people, upon AA, indeed, upon any set of circumstances whatsoever. Then only could I be free to love as Francis had.

Emotional and instinctual satisfactions, I saw, were really the extra dividends of having love, offering love, and expressing a love appropriate to each relation of life...

Thus I think it can work out with emotional sobriety. If we examine every disturbance we have, great or small, we will find at the root of it some unhealthy dependency and its consequent unhealthy demand. Let us, with God's help, continually surrender these hobbling demands. Then we can be set free to live and love; we may then be able to Twelfth Step ourselves and others into emotional sobriety.

In the article Bill points us to the solution via the same Twelve Steps of AA, but applied at a much deeper level—a progressive application. He directs us toward the core of our personality, that which the Big Book labels "old ideas" and "causes and conditions." This makes sense when we connect back to a foundational principle of the program of recovery, that somehow the process must produce a "psychic change," a substantially altered mental, psychological and emotional state, which can only occur deep within our being.

It's useful to realize that emotional sobriety is not merely the management of one's emotions, which is quite frankly a fool's game. When emotions surge, we lack power over them in the same way that we lack power over alcohol, drugs and many other forms of addiction. Instead we are pointed to root causes, the underlying dependencies from which emotional upsets emerge. When those are resolved, emotional sobriety falls upon us. We are struck emotionally sober in the same way that many of us were struck physically sober.

A Commentary on The Twelve Steps of Alcoholics Anonymous

The Twelve Steps of Alcoholics Anonymous have a storied history and have been adapted into any number of forms. Whether you are alcoholic or not, or whether you have some other kind of addiction, they have proven to be effective and resilient for many.

1. We admitted we were powerless over alcohol—that our lives had become unmanageable.
2. Came to believe that a Power greater than ourselves could restore us to sanity.
3. Made a decision to turn our will and our lives over to the care of God as we understood God.
4. Made a searching and fearless moral inventory of ourselves.
5. Admitted to God, to ourselves, and to another human being the exact nature of our wrongs.
6. Were entirely ready to have God remove all these defects of character.
7. Humbly asked God to remove our shortcomings.
8. Made a list of all persons we had harmed, and became willing to make amends to them all.

9. Made direct amends to such people wherever possible, except when to do so would injure them or others.

10. Continued to take personal inventory, and when we were wrong, promptly admitted it.

11. Sought through prayer and meditation to improve our conscious contact with God *as we understood God*, praying only for knowledge of God's will for us and the power to carry that out.

12. Having had a spiritual awakening as the result of these steps, we tried to carry this message to other alcoholics, and to practice these principles in all our affairs.

For many it is useful to think about the Twelve Steps a little differently. This is so because for some the religious language is off-putting, and for others the stiltedness of the language can be problematic. Here is another way to think of the steps as the solution to the problem of alcoholism or other addictions:

- For reasons that are not clear, we do not have the means to solve our addiction. We suffer from a lack of power. (Step One)

- We are told by others that there is power that is available to us. Call it God, or a Higher Power, or Higher Self, or the Force. Regardless of the name and our beliefs, there is power in which we come to believe, a power that is greater than ourselves. (Steps Two and Three)

- What is it that blocks us off from that power? Let us explore and get a good look at the underlying causes and conditions in our lives and within us that block power from flowing. (Steps Four and Five)

- Since we cannot solve our problems because we lack access to power, we ask for help. Ask a Higher Power, or a group of recovering people, or a therapist for assistance in revealing and addressing the blocks to power. (Steps Six and Seven)
- Set about to identify and make right the behaviors, actions, guilts and shames that are the result of being blocked off from power. Participate in the solution in every way we possibly can. (Steps Eight and Nine)
- Continue, continue, continue to watch for the indications that power is being blocked, whether through action or inaction, and even through the ways in which we perceive ourselves and our worlds. Do whatever is needed to address them as they arise. (Step Ten, which is essentially a repetition of the principles in Steps Four through Nine.)
- With prayer, contemplation, meditation or any other useful means, seek to make contact with the source of the power that is needed. (Step Eleven)
- Practice these principles in every way possible and pass it on whenever possible. Simultaneously, enjoy the benefits of the access to power with all the benefits it brings. (Step Twelve)

To summarize, we have a lack of power because we are blocked off from it. Therefore, we take the necessary steps to clear the inner channel and keep it unobstructed so that power can flow and solve our problems. This is the heart of a psychic change sufficient to transform us.

Setting the Scene

*We are only operating a spiritual kindergarten in which
people are enabled to get over drinking and find the grace
to go on living to better effect. Each man's theology has to
be his own quest, his own affair.*

—BILL WILSON

Perhaps the best wisdom and encouragement I ever received
in recovery came from Betsy Comstock. She passed away a
number of years ago, but she had achieved long-term sobriety after a terrible relapse. It was a moment in my first year
of sobriety when I was suddenly aware of how daunting was
the prospect of staying sober over time. I was terrified of
what I faced, so I asked Betsy how she managed in the face
of the likelihood of getting drunk.

"Ron," she began after a long lapse to collect her thoughts,
"You'll hear so many people tell you so many things you
must do, and I can't disagree with practicing the Twelve
Steps, taking full advantage of a sponsor and professional
help, working with others to find their own recovery, and
service work with and for others. But it seems to me you
have to continue to be willing to grow along spiritual lines."

I promptly jumped into commenting, and Betsy hushed

me. "Honey, don't think for a moment you have any idea what it means to grow along spiritual lines. There is no telling what will come your way."

Not only are there unexpected elements in anyone's spirituality, most certainly there are factors far beyond not drinking and not drugging. Here are a few of those to set the scene for an exploration of Progressive Recovery through the Twelve Steps.

In the years since the founding of Alcoholics Anonymous much has been learned about addiction. While it does not conflict with the principles in the Twelve Steps, it adds much to our understanding.

There is little question today that some of the roots of addiction are in the human physiology. Much research into the neurology of the brain, metabolic functioning, blood chemistry, and nutrition confirms there are factors occurring in the body that contribute to the likelihood of addiction becoming activated in someone. While there is yet much debate about which factors and by what mechanisms, there is widespread agreement that addiction is in part a reflection of the dynamics of the body.

There is likewise strong evidence that the nature of addiction is progressive. Something within the physiology of the human body makes for the likelihood that once an addiction begins it will probably worsen without intervention. While there are any number of proponents for moderation strategies, the consensus would seem to be that abstinence is the most likely path to success.

What about psychopharmacology, mental health treatment and therapeutic interventions? No one with a reasonably good knowledge of addiction would discount any of these as useful. In fact, many would argue for having a recovery sponsor or coach, a therapist, an addictionologist, and a spiritual counselor, each with a black-belt in their respective practices.

That said, it does seem to be consistently true that all of these are much more effective when abstinence is in full force. As is often heard in the rooms of recovery, most anything will become worse in the presence of alcohol, drugs and other addictive substances or processes.

An evolving understanding of childhood stress and trauma[1], and attachment disorder[2] is revealing that these too can be contributors to addiction. Some of the techniques being practiced in trauma mitigation are proving to be very effective. And on the fringes of the recovery field, we find the use of psychotropic substances and practices to be useful for some[3]. These include the African hallucinogen ibogaine, South American ayahuasca, Shamanic practices in soul retrieval, and breath work. All these seem to have a capacity to potentially address underlying psychic disconnect. Of course, given the nature of addiction, any exploration into these areas should be approached with great caution.

In recent years, research has also suggested that the opposite of addiction is connection, that humans in the throes of addictions of all kinds suffer from a depreciated sense of themselves and from emotional and social isolation[4]. While there is no doubt that community and human interaction is an important ingredient in long-term recovery, there are ample examples of those with connection who remain unable to find sobriety. And while we applaud new models that seek to create sober lifestyles, so too do these appear to be insufficient in and of themselves.

It should also be noted that our evolving understanding now allows us to include process addictions such as gambling, codependency and love addiction. And to acknowledge that these latter two can and do run deeply in the lives of those who are in Al-Anon family recovery, and Adult Children of Alcoholics (ACA). It seems the effects of alcoholism and addiction are unlimited in the ways in which they can appear in the lives of those affected.

None of these factors are to be discounted. However, it is clear that addiction is much more than a behavioral or moral problem. Indeed, cycles of guilt and shame that emanate from failure, judgment and punishment seem only to exacerbate or accelerate addictions.

Clearly, we are faced with a complex phenomenon. Those in the field would agree the treatment of addiction can be exceedingly complicated. At the same time, there is strong evidence from the underpinnings of Alcoholics Anonymous on a factor that cannot be excluded. Carl Jung suggested in his assessment of alcoholism that in the absence of some kind of "psychic change" there was little hope of recovery. He understood what would eventually be described as a "lack of power" being the underlying problem, and that nothing but a "transforming experience of the spirit" could suffice for recovery.

The Greeks called this psychic change metanoia, which for our purposes translates as a profound change of heart. We know it has taken place when there is a sudden and dramatic change of behavior. Some in recovery from alcoholism refer to this as being struck sober. It can also be seen when after much inner work a character defect is altered in a surprising way, the solution seeming to fall upon the person without obvious cause. The whole point of this process of spiritual recovery is to produce metanoia, a psychic change sufficient to produce a transformation.

It is our contention in Progressive Recovery that something significant must disrupt the addict's way of being, their frame of reference to themselves. Whatever the mix may prove to be for any addict, it will need to be substantive. And for many, it will need to persist and progress over time. In the absence of progressivity in recovery, the progressivity of the addiction can overtake the recovering person.

Progressive Recovery means a continuing and deepening practice of the Twelve Steps, sometimes in nontraditional ways. This allows us to discover and release the underlying causes and conditions. That release permits "Power" to flow, and healing to occur. The result is a progressive restoration to sanity and wholeness.

The Twelve Steps—
Practiced Progressively

This Shit Has Got to Stop

I'm only as honest as my dishonesty will allow,
as willing as unwillingness permits, and as open-minded
as a closed mind can be.
—RONALD CHAPMAN

᠔

In the beginning, we have to see there is a problem. This is not to say we simply know it in our heads, rather that we begin to experience sufficient pain or suffering to get our attention. It's worth noting that sometimes clarity can come without pain or suffering, or we can nudge ourselves toward it with information and learning. (We'll talk more about that in a moment.)

Let's be honest though. As one man in recovery observed, "We rarely see the light, though we do often feel the heat." It seems we often need the heat of discomfort to make us teachable enough that we can see the light.

In fact, that is how our ego is constructed—to stabilize and maintain a status quo right up until the moment that we understand something must change in our reality. From a psychic point of view, this tendency of the ego to resist change probably keeps us from perishing as the result of taking unnecessary risks. Furthermore, it very well could be that this effect of defending a status quo keeps us from fully seeing the reality of our circumstances, which could be overwhelming to us. Regardless, we each have an ego that is resistant to change. That means denial and delusion are part of the normal human experience.

Until we see there is a terrible problem, until something bypasses the egoic framework, we simply do not need or want anything to be different. Without the clarity of a problem in us and our lives that needs solving, we won't even look for a solution. And without discomfort sufficient to propel us toward reality, we simply cannot engage the problem.

Thus, we begin Progressive Recovery with Step Zero: This shit has got to stop.

Beyond getting clean and sober, as each next challenge arises on the path of our recovery, we will have to experience another Step Zero. This reality is so common that we often hear people in recovery refer to "another fucking opportunity for growth." It is a classic story that an addict puts down their drug of choice only to find new ones. Abstinence from alcohol reveals the need to abstain from some other drugs, which reveals the need to deal with food and sugar, which reveals the need to quit smoking, which reveals the need to overcome something else, over and over again. Yet each hurdle can only be overcome with another realization that the newest problem is intolerable.

Some would call Step Zero "hitting bottom." But it's more than an external breakdown, it is an internal moment of clarity that produces a willingness that is simply unexplainable.

As an example, consider Jim. (Also known as the "Voice" for his powerful sports announcer voice. The recovery rooms love nicknames, since last names are often unknown in the service of anonymity: Belt Buckle Johnny, Theresa Blonde, Be Bop Tony, Crazy Jane, and so on.) Jim was a long-time sober member of AA, a powerful communicator about recovery, and well-versed in the Twelve Steps. He also had a lifelong tobacco addiction about which he would announce, "I did not get sober because I had a problem with Pall Mall shorts."

One day at his home group Jim was quite somber. When called upon he said, "I was wrong, and I need to admit it. I was so full of myself, and so addicted to nicotine, I just had to say that crap. But I have lung cancer and next week they are going to remove one of my lungs." He shook his head and his eyes were rimmed with tears. "I did come to AA to quit smoking because it's killing me. I haven't had a cigarette in a week, and the Twelve Steps work on that too."

That is the sound of Step Zero—an awakening, a moment of Seeing True™. And with that comes some kind of access to power to act, access to a power that was formerly not available.

Sometimes Step Zero can take years. We just can't see the problem. Attribute it to denial or delusion if you like. Or maybe we simply have not yet been sufficiently tenderized by suffering.

As I mentioned in my story that began this book, at five years in sobriety I remarried. In short order it became clear to me that I was in way over my head with relationships and parenting. Within two years I was suffering terribly. My longest serving sponsor suggested I needed inpatient treatment for codependency and love addiction. I was unconvinced, certain I could manage well enough.

At 17 years sober, a decade later, I called him and announced, "You were right. I need to go for inpatient treatment." One more relationship had gone awry and I could no longer refuse to see that I needed professional intervention.

Thankfully, he was indeed wise and had no need to shame me about my delay. "Well we wouldn't want to rush these things," he said gently.

With many of us, it is the second or third or fourth Step Zero that catapults us into Progressive Recovery, which can take 10, 12 or even 20 years. It takes what it takes. Commonly we hear people describe the many things they are doing as part of their program of recovery, much of which is both appropriate and useful. Still, we hear them admit they have somehow become stuck, and do not seem to be able to find the next level of the solution.

While suffering as a precursor to Step Zero is not uncommon, there is ample evidence that with continuing processes of inquiry we can raise the depths of our Step Zero. We can engage in therapy, ongoing journaling, and other explorations with ourselves and others in any number of settings, from churches to study groups. It is typical to hear of much spiritual or philosophical fruit being borne from years of effort that preceded sobriety, a blossoming that merely awaited the last drink or drug. If we engage ourselves and our lives, there is reason to believe we can avoid the heat and actually see the light. Suffering really may be optional. Yet if suffering proves to be essential for anyone to find their way to Step Zero, it is completely understandable given the baffling nature of addiction.

Even if we don't manage to do better, even if we must experience great pain and suffering, there is tremendous hope in understanding the elegance and beauty of life's design.

Consider the movie *Groundhog Day*, which some believe to be a powerful spiritual or philosophical parable. The main character, Phil, played by Bill Murray, lives the same day over and over and over again until he learns what he needs to learn in order to move on. We are designed to learn, and life is designed to teach. Every apparent misstep, every moment of heartache, every distraction or delay merely increases the likelihood of an impending moment of clarity that will transform us. At best this understanding allows us to be thankful for each Step Zero, and with that acceptance, we become more graceful learners.

Before we conclude this exploration of Step Zero, let's flush out some mischief regarding free will.

Here's what our culture likes to believe:

We profess that each of us has the ability to choose. There is no point in engaging in what is often called "the debating society" in the rooms of recovery because thinkers and philosophers and wise ones have been arguing this matter for generations without resolution. Instead we need only look to the evidence around us.

If it's true we have free will, then we must conclude that every circumstance in our lives is present because we have knowingly chosen it. That means that every mistake, every terrible outcome, every aspect of our lives was the result of a conscious and deliberate intention. Literally we must then accept that we have chosen to do what we've done in our lives and to be exactly who we are. One honest look within ourselves at our reality will show this cannot be true. It is the rare individual who acts out of conscious and ill intent. The only question we can seriously entertain is why and how such things come to pass when we are often not even aware of them. That is a matter for the next chapter on powerlessness.

But before we turn our attention forward, it is useful to acknowledge that the one benefit of believing in the power to choose is that it provides us cause for judgment and condemnation. The human ego and society love having justification, including self-blame.

The guilt and shame that emerge from a cycle of fault-finding merely contribute to the downward spiral of addiction. Of course, with a little bit of enlightenment, we can also acknowledge that even this can aid in attaining the breakthrough of Step Zero.

There is a great beauty in becoming teachable. The suffering, hitting bottom, and being sick and tired of being sick and tired are valuable when they aid us in finally getting done and truly acknowledging "this shit has got to stop."

A Toolkit for a Progressive Step Zero

Let's first admit that some of us may need pain, suffering and consequences to open our hearts and minds. While we should not wish that upon anyone, sometimes it is true for us.

Assuming we would like to avoid that unfortunate path, that we would like to see the light of a deeper recovery rather than feel the heat of more pain and suffering, the magic elixir for Step Zero is information that leads to awareness that in turn leads to a moment of clarity. There are countless ways to engage in fact-finding. Here are a few that we've found to be useful:

- There is no substitute for telling the truth about our circumstances. Admittedly we may be unable to see the truth, in which case we'll simply need to do the best we can. Being honest that we may not be able to tell the truth has been known to be sufficient.
- There is nothing more effective than owning our own reality. We would urge you to do everything in your power to stop focusing on what you believe to be the external causes of your suffering. No matter the appearances, it is very clear that our problems are within us, not outside of us, though we are usually not aware of them.
- Many of us have found an opening within ourselves by attending Twelve Step meetings even when it is against our will. Merely being exposed can open us up to clarity about the disease of alcoholism or addiction.
- If we are feeling particularly bold, and we are able to see there is a problem, we ask others who are affected by the problem we are unwilling to address to tell us how they are affected. That will often penetrate the ego and crack us open. It will not be comfortable, but it may prove to be priceless.
- For most any addiction or life challenge, there are ample resources online or in libraries. Start reading.

Start assessing. Anything we can do to force some information into ourselves will not be in vain, but try not to get stuck in self-help alone.

- So too with anything we can write about the consequences, the effect on others, the pros and cons. That information displaces the misinformation that otherwise governs. Journaling is a powerful tool.

- We can go to a therapist. Or to a spiritual advisor. Or to a trusted friend and begin to explore. Try to tell them the truth.

- There is always prayer. "Help" is a very good one, and simple too. One particularly effective affirmation is: "Thank you for allowing me to feel what I need to feel, see what I need to see, and learn what I need to learn." Whether it is God that is responding, or Higher Self, or the Soul, or Angels, or the Force, is immaterial. Asking for help tends to be fruitful.

- As much as possible seek to be curious. Whenever possible, set aside judgments, blame and condemnation.

- While we do not intend to be critical of the rooms of recovery, sometimes when we are long in recovery, the feedback in the rooms will actually minimize our problems and discourage inquiry. It is useful to remember that all of us have fears and can go to great lengths to avoid them, which sometimes includes discouraging others from exploring matters which are a threat to us. Whenever possible, seek out people and places that support inquiry and exploration.

But what if we're in denial and cannot see something?

Truthfully, if we cannot see—we cannot see. However, anything we can do to seek out information will be useful.

Regardless, we can trust the addiction to get our attention. If we can act in a way that makes that easier, that is simply beautiful. We would always wish any of us a higher bottom. At the same time, we will fully support the suffering needed to open someone up, allow information to flow, and set the scene for transformation.

Remember that the principle of Step Zero applies at all junctures in our recovery. It is essential to face alcoholism or addiction, and likewise necessary for every additional element of sobriety or emotional sobriety as we seek and grow.

Into Action with Step Zero

In a journal, consider the following questions regarding Step Zero: (We will often refer to journaling because we have found it to be very helpful. Please obtain a journal or notebook that you will use specifically for your Progressive Recovery work.)

- Describe a problem with which you have been struggling. Choose something that is truly intolerable. Be as honest as you are able in describing it. If you are new to recovery from alcoholism or addiction, start there. If you have already found your way into recovery from your primary addiction, perhaps you now have a gambling or shopping problem, or some kind of relationship or sex addiction. Maybe you are angry, or violent, or neglectful to loved ones. Or it may be that you have chronic employment problems. Telling the truth about ourselves and our struggles is a powerful tool.

- Now describe at length the benefits you seem to get from it: Does it somehow make you feel better about yourself, or your life? Do you receive some kind of unusual personal reward from it? Does it somehow let you off the hook? Could it be that you simply don't really know a better way, and this is all you know? If you can't see the apparent benefits, imagine what they might be. We do nothing without some payoff, no matter how strange or twisted.

- Now consider the consequences: Does your situation undermine relationships? How? Is your employment affected? In what ways? Are there financial implications? What is the likely true cost to you? Where are you unable to spend useful time as a result of the problem? What are the opportunities lost? Do you feel regret, guilt or shame? Do you somehow act it out upon others?

- What might be the underlying causes? Do you see a pattern in your life and history with this problem? Are there particular people or types of people who are part of it? Particular places or circumstances? Even if it is not clear to you what the cause may be, try depersonalizing—why would someone like you want to do this?

- Who would be a safe person with which to discuss this Step Zero? A sponsor or spiritual advisor? A trusted friend? If these people would not be open-minded enough, or have enough insight or awareness, do you know a therapist or other professional who could assist?

If not, who do you know who could make a good refer-
ral? Remember, left to our own devices we are typically
unable to see our way clear. We need a fresh set of eyes.

- What Twelve Step meeting have you attended, or have
  you heard about where you have reason to believe you
  could be open and honest about the problem? If you do
  not have any ideas, who can you ask for guidance to
  find a community that can support you? Remember,
  many of us are so-called double, triple and quadruple
  winners—we often belong to multiple programs of
  recovery, some of which may not even be based on the
  Twelve Steps.

- If you are feeling particularly bold, can you ask others
  who are affected to tell you about how they experience
  it? Can you be willing to hear such information from
  another person? If not someone close to the issue, can
  you find another person to share their thoughts about
  how it might affect others?

- What resources might be helpful? Do you have access to
  a library with a librarian who can refer you? Have you
  explored the issue online? What books, assessments or
  tools do you know which can help with information
  gathering?

- Now tell yourself about the degree of your willingness.
  Be honest. Note the things you are willing to do as
  well as those you are unwilling to do to move forward.
  Now consider the causes of unwillingness. Why do
  you hold back? What would it take to convince you?
  To what lengths are you willing to go?

Powerlessness

Step One
We admitted we were powerless over alcohol—
that our lives had become unmanageable.

۶ٯ

The fact is that if you're truly powerless, you're doomed.
And that's the point really ... Twelve Step recovery is
not self-help ... At the root of the Twelve Steps is the
notion that you can't help yourself, and trying to do so
only gets you deeper into your addiction.
—RAMI SHAPIRO

۶ٯ

Once Step Zero convinces us there is a problem, it's useful
to understand that problem fully. And it's even better to
understand we don't have the power to fix it. Let's begin to
understand by exploring the principle of admission.

It is not uncommon to hear someone in recovery say, "I
knew for years I had a problem." Yet we must distinguish

between information, knowing and understanding. How do we get data from our heads to our hearts?

Somehow the implications of information we receive must penetrate and become understanding. Sometimes that comes from an emotional experience, though it can also come as a result of diligent exploration.

Let's use Bonnie's experience with her alcoholic father and the effect it had on her as a demonstration of the impact of an emotional experience.

Bonnie's dad was a chronic alcoholic, which she had observed for years. As a nurse practicing in emergency rooms, Bonnie was well equipped to see and understand. But one day, after an especially long shift that had drained her, she came home to find her mother sobbing and distressed. Her dad was drunk and had been berating her mom.

Bonnie snapped. She went into his bedroom where he lay on the bed awake but intoxicated. She didn't say a word. Instead she went to his closet and took his handgun from the shelf. Silently she loaded the weapon.

Then she turned to her dad and said simply, "Daddy, get up and get in the car."

Not surprisingly he was suddenly quite sober. "Honey, what are you doing with my gun?"

"Daddy, get in the goddamned car."

"Honey," he repeated, "what are you doing?"

Bonnie began to cry. Between sobs she managed to say, "We are so tired of this shit, Daddy. I'm going to take you out into the desert and leave you there with your gun. I want you to just blow your head off and put us all out of your misery."

Bonnie's breakdown was the catalyst for her father's

sobriety, the beginning of his long-term recovery. As an aspect of Bonnie's story, her moment of stark clarity helped her understand the full implications of the alcoholism she had known about for years. She was shaken from her complacency, which in turn projected the implication upon her dad. And that raw emotion and those full implications broke through his denial and allowed information to penetrate deeply into him. The result was a transformation for both of them.

Obviously, we would never wish such a horrific story on anyone. However, Bonnie's story is not an isolated occurrence; the rooms of recovery are filled with terrible and tragic stories that changed people's lives. Understanding the implications of alcoholism can fall upon us through the power of emotions. This then can create an opening for admission, or to paraphrase AA's Big Book, admitting it to our innermost selves.

The twelve-step rooms are also filled with countless stories of tragedy that were insufficient to create understanding and admission. Some of these tales end in death, insanity or incarceration. We do not know what might break through to awaken us to reality, only that something must come to pass to produce a psychic change, a new mental and emotional state sufficient to allow for real progress and greater sobriety to follow.

A more typical process to admission is an educational one. That's the approach in AA's Big Book. It seeks to explain the nature of the problem as "lack of power," not alcohol, thus we are powerless. Then it proceeds to offer four ways that we can be without power.

The first is denial. We cannot even see there is a problem. It simply cannot be acknowledged. Thus, there is no power and no option other than to continue in one's addiction.

The second is what is described as a "strange mental blank spot." Literally we cannot recall the moment that preceded the first drink or drug. A compulsion acts upon us against our will. There is no awareness, and thus no power.

The third is a never-ending debate with oneself that always ends the same way: with a drink or a drug. There is insufficient means to talk ourselves out of the substance and thus powerlessness rules.

The fourth is capitulation. We simply stop trying because we have failed so many times. Again, this is a form of powerlessness.

Wayne Liquorman wrote an entire book that explored the problem. *The Way of Powerlessness* walks the reader through the Twelve Steps with reference after reference after reference to powerlessness.

> Unfortunately, the question of powerlessness is rarely simple. It is complicated by the fact that from time to time we have the appearance of control. We have the thought, "I don't think I'll engage in my addictive behavior today" and then we don't engage in it ... The fact that on a hundred other occasions we had the same intention, but acted contrary to our intent, isn't even considered ...

In short ... somehow, we do not have the ability to act in our own best interests, thus we are powerless over the first drink. Once we start, we can never predict when it will end because once we have the first drink, more drinks will invariably follow.

While powerlessness is difficult to see, unmanageability is much easier. Every recovering person has a seemingly endless number of stories about how one drink, drug or behavior became many, and produced carnage throughout their lives: incarceration, broken relationships, unemployment, homelessness, car wrecks, deaths, and more.

Simply enough, it is the failure to see the problem as a lack of power to choose that underlies it all.

Progressive Recovery proposes that we must understand the nature of the problem. We must somehow find a way to internalize this devastating reality—that in every given moment we are without defense unless somehow power can be tapped, and that power must come from somewhere other than us because the evidence is clear that we are simply unable to be the solution.

Progressive Recovery then proposes that we will necessarily find that the principle of powerlessness can be seen in any number of places in our lives. After we stop drinking or drugging, we'll likely see tobacco addictions that are killing us. Or food addictions and disorders. Or process addictions like gambling or sex. Or relational addictions like codependency and love addiction. Some of us will even find we have managed to become addicted to things that seem innocuous or virtuous. There are many who are surprised that they are addicted to caffeine, or even non-narcotic, non-addictive medicines. Some discover that their escape into television or exercise is destroying relationships. There is seemingly no limit to the possible ways in which our emotional, psychological or physical addiction can undermine us.

Next, Progressive Recovery asks us to find a way to get this information into our awareness and then into our understanding. We must digest the information and assimilate it into our being. Only then can we see the wisdom of the words of Maya Angelou, "I did then what I knew how to do. Now that I know better, I do better." She was not referring to having information in our heads, rather that the information has become understanding.

Often we must back ourselves into understanding our powerlessness by inventorying the unmanageability in our lives. For example, Denny could not see that his sex addiction was destroying his life in sobriety. It was only when he tallied the many broken relationships, the estrangement from his children, the arrests for soliciting prostitutes, and ultimately his two slips in sobriety caused by sex-fueled shame, that he was able to finally admit powerlessness. He would later say, "I was just not willing to give up my sexing until I could see all the bullshit it caused."

Let's close by admitting that the notion of powerlessness is deeply disturbing. At first most of us can only see it in the context of the specific addiction, which brought us to the point of beginning. Yet once that is addressed, we are forced to examine the problem of lack of power over and over again. Many of us cling to an insistence that we have the power to choose in other addictive arenas. Sooner or later, most of us will progress beyond that perspective. The disease of addiction will teach us.

When we finally begin to examine the many possible

ways that sobriety can still be compromised beyond a drink or a drug, and when we look fully at both powerlessness and unmanageability, eventually understanding will penetrate. Then the power of admission will take over, and with it will come willingness. Said a wise elder in recovery, "If you're not yet willing, you haven't yet looked deeply enough."

A Toolkit for a Progressive Step One

As noted in the preceding paragraphs, a progressive approach to powerlessness will likely involve some effort on our part. While addictions will likely hammer upon us, engaging and exploring the problems are our best strategies. Here are a few tools we have found useful:

- Journaling or written inventory is always helpful, especially if it is performed on a continuing basis. This is true whether we write about the incidents and proof of powerlessness, or the indications of unmanageability. It doesn't seem to matter how we record this valuable information, only that we do so. Capturing items in writing seems to increase our understanding, but most certainly increases our awareness.
- The Big Book, *Alcoholics Anonymous*, can be a very useful tool simply by studying the introductory chapters and substituting the newest addiction for alcohol. However, merely reading the text does not seem to deepen our understanding. Instead, borrow from what generations of teachers have taught: a notebook for notes and a highlighter for the book.

- *The Way of Powerlessness* by Wayne Liquorman can be a challenging book. By studying it, taking notes, and examining our reality, we will be forced to confront the issue head-on.
- *Recovery-The Sacred Art: The Twelve Steps as Spiritual Practice* by Rami Shapiro illustrates a deep understanding of the problem of powerlessness. It's another useful resource for study and contemplation.
- *Escape from Intimacy: Untangling the "Love Addictions"— Sex, Romance, Relationship* by Anne Wilson Schaef deeply explores the problems reflected in relationships for people in recovery, and even for those not in recovery. For many, there is much valuable exploration in this realm.
- A number of works by Pia Mellody and Melody Beattie have been extremely useful to many who come to see the need for recovery from some form of relational addiction.
- As always, there is no substitute for talking these matters through with a sponsor, a therapist, an advisor or a trusted friend. Journaling can be a powerful complement to these conversations.

Into Action with Step One

In your journal, consider the following questions regarding Step One. Please note some of these items may feel repetitive after your work on Step Zero. Sometimes it takes many repetitions before we break through our own lack of seeing and understanding. Because of that, we urge you to persist.

- Review your notes and thoughts related to Step Zero.

Has more been revealed to you about the nature of the problem(s) you are now facing beyond your initial alcoholism or addiction? Feel free to embellish on your thinking, and as always, seek to be as honest with yourself as possible.

- Now as we suggested earlier, let's see if we can back into greater awareness of our powerlessness by accounting for unmanageability. What is proving difficult or impossible for you to control or manage? What recent situations demonstrate unmanageability? What have you tried to do to manage well? To what degree has it worked? Be honest. How do you feel about yourself and your efforts?

- Let's take the Big Book approach to lack of power.
  - » First, can you see signs that you are in denial of the problem? Do you have some justification or explanation that allows you to avoid looking at your powerlessness? Or are there other behaviors or activities that merely distract you from facing yourself? Can you see how these amount to a lack of power?
  - » Secondly, do you have evidence of a strange mental blank spot? When you look very closely at what precedes the problem emerging, or the behavior beginning, do you have a lapse where there is simply no power to choose? Does this make sense to you as a lack of access to power to do or be different?
  - » The third instance of powerlessness is the endless debate with yourself that you never really manage to win. Do you argue with yourself about the behavior or compulsion? What rationale do you use to convince

yourself you have some power? What is the evidence that your arguments with yourself fail?

» Fourth and last, have you capitulated to the problem? Have you simply ceased trying to manage? Have you given up? How does it feel to admit to yourself that you are failing to solve the problem yourself?

- Remember, each of us experiences lack of power in different ways. Not all four ways of powerlessness may apply. Regardless, go back now to reading in the Big Book or your preferred resource. What else can you see about the state of your powerlessness?

- How willing do you now seem to be to admit the nature of the failure of your will and self-management strategies? Do you feel like you've exhausted your means to solve the problem? What would it now take to admit to yourself, to a power greater than yourself, and another human being that you are without choice in dealing with your problem(s)? Are you convinced enough to proceed to the following steps?

Finding Power

Step Two
Came to believe that a power greater than ourselves
could restore us to sanity.

Step Three
Made a decision to turn our will and our lives over
to the care of God as we understood God.

ॐ

Find any wise path.
The way is made with every step.
—RONALD CHAPMAN

ॐ

Let's be honest. These two steps are initially "God-steps" for most everyone. And because of that, they can present all kinds of challenges. There is no small amount of historical grievance from many people who have suffered at the hands of religion or its representatives. Yet in the end, most of those who find recovery somehow reconcile themselves with what is generally called a "Higher Power," which is often misperceived as a code phrase for God.

We'll make no attempt to revisit what many people have navigated in the way of a Higher Power, rather we'll explore how this idea fits into our emerging Progressive Recovery framework.

To summarize our exploration thus far: things are intolerable, and they can't continue. This shit has got to stop. While we may be free from our primary addiction, new problems are emerging despite being clean and sober. Yet for reasons unclear, we lack the power to solve new problems. We are powerless. Worse still, no matter what we do, the carnage only seems to grow around us. Somehow, we're going to have to find power and commit to it. This won't come from any sense of virtue, but rather out of bleak necessity. We've seen we are without defense if left to our own devices. We understand the problem well enough to have arrived at facing the notion that a Higher Power is needed.

This wisdom tells us to let go and let something bigger than us take over. It can be anything we want as long as it's greater than us. After all, there is no evidence we are going to be successful on our own.

That point bears a comment that will illuminate something strange we see in the rooms of recovery. The language of Step Two doesn't use the word "God." Instead it says it must be something greater than ourselves. Of course! We can't demonstrate the power, so we must turn to something larger than us to supply that power. And it can be anything as long as we don't think we are that power.

This is a brilliant point in the Twelve Steps. Suddenly we see why it is that Methodists, and Catholics, and Buddhists, and Hindus, and Sufis, and most anyone else can get sober. Even those who decide to use "good orderly direction" or "group of drunks" (acronyms for GOD) and even those who profess atheism or agnosticism find access to power. It doesn't matter what we believe in, only that we no longer believe we possess sufficient power of our own. If we are sufficiently convinced that we cannot supply the power and that there is something greater than us that does, it will be sufficient.

This is a point worth repeating. The reason atheists and agnostics can get sober is not because they believe in God, but because they have abandoned the idea that they can solve their problems by themselves. Therefore, what we believe about what we will call "Progressive Power" is not important. It only matters that we've ceased to believe in ourselves as the solution.

Many will be agitated by this suggestion because of an attachment to our particular God concept or beliefs. This is a progressive proposition. In Progressive Recovery, our conception of the Progressive Power continues to grow larger. It turns out that the restoration to sanity promised in Step Two is a progressively growing sanity observed Al C., an alcoholic in long-term recovery. At any point in time there is more restoration available to us. But it is predicated on finding more power than heretofore we have been able to access. This is a remarkable idea.

So too is it remarkable to understand that as long as we desire greater restoration, we will need to seek and find a

Progressive Power. This will cause our conception and clarity to advance, and with it our sanity and sobriety.

We often hear that addiction is a progressive disease, that it only gets worse even when we are not actively in addiction. Certainly, we would need Progressive Recovery.

There is tremendous unrealized potential in spiritual recovery no matter where we stand in that process. When we can engage the next layer of addiction and dysfunction within us, and find increasing access to power, we can achieve greater and greater restoration.

It goes without saying that the decision we make to allow that Progressive Power to act must be renewed and deepened, over and over and over again. It is a progressive decision.

There is a particular phrase the Big Book uses several times that is well worth considering—"being convinced." Being convinced that we are powerless brings us deeply into Step One. Being convinced that we are not able to be the solution because we lack sufficient power brings us to the threshold of Step Three. Yet what does it take to be convinced?

We need evidence. We need data, information, anecdotes, stories, experience and anything else that will lead us to an understanding sufficient to allow us to move forward. To use a phrase from the Big Book, we have to see "the hopelessness and futility of life as we have been living it." And in Progressive Recovery, this will be realized over and over and over again as we confront each next layer of our dysfunction, compulsions and addictions.

If we become stuck at some point, we are going to need more evidence in every imaginable form. If we find ourselves balking in this effort to find power, we may need to return again to inventory or journaling, spiritual and recovery advisors, and therapy too. An inability to move forward or a lack of success likely suggests that we must go back to fact-finding and exploration. As my longest-serving sponsor says, "If you can't be willing, look for the source of your unwillingness." When it is revealed and released, willingness will not present a problem.

Another element that is important to this process of turning things over to Progressive Power comes in seeing that it works in others. We need evidence that there is a solution available to us. And seeing others demonstrating progressive recovery is a reassurance to us.

However, before moving forward, let's briefly talk about reality in the rooms of recovery.

Those of us in the rooms invariably have terrible histories with feeling a part of community. Our unknown or unspoken fears of exclusion make it difficult to tell the truth of our present circumstances.

There's a story heard in the rooms in any number of forms. It's the story of a woman who we will call Barb.

Two recovering people enter a meeting and are greeted by Margaret, who has clearly been crying. "Did you hear about Barb?" she asks.

The two women are surprised. "We just saw her earlier in the week. She sounded great."

"I know," said Margaret. "Barb got drunk yesterday. Twenty years sober. I don't get it."

These are the stories of those who have become stuck, though they may not even know it. It is not a sign of an inadequate recovery. It may be a sign of an inability to speak of it. Regardless, it is certainly an indicator of a need for Progressive Recovery. It tells us that something within us has been exposed or revealed, something we could not previously see that now needs attention via the Twelve Steps.

Emerging challenges are not a sign of a poor program of recovery. They are the product of cumulative recovery that reveals a next degree of healing that is needed. Success in recovery comes with successive revelation of what next efforts are required.

Yet because of our fears, the tendency toward denial, or to minimize, or to bypass, is quite great. It is these unresolved matters that are sometimes at the heart of a relapse or even suicide in recovery.

As we noted earlier, the conditions for a progressive Step Two and Step Three are that we must be convinced that something must be addressed, and we must also see evidence from someone or something that provides direction and hope. Regrettably, we are often ill prepared for what emerges to be healed as recovery progresses. At worst, we face three possible conclusions when something emerges within us or our lives, usually with a fairly large degree of murkiness.

- Everyone around who is professing to be "happy, joyous and free" is lying. Since we are troubled, failing or suffering, and we cannot believe that others might lie, we are unable to reconcile our very real experiences.
- The Twelve Steps must not actually work as advertised. We have clear evidence they are not working for us, and yet we hear and perhaps believe they do work. Still we are trapped by our own experiences.

- What emerges then seems to prove there is something wrong with us that is irreparable. Sadly, this is often our conclusion.

For all intents and purpose, we lose faith when in fact the problem is that we don't know how to proceed. Something new is presenting itself for our attention, and we do not know how to work with it via the Twelve Steps. No one has taught us how to work more deeply on our recovery, we've possibly heard little in the rooms of recovery about our dilemma, and we may not realize we need professional help. Of course, if we have long-term recovery and are struggling, we may be all the more likely to find fault with ourselves.

To repeat, the sign of new challenges emerging is in fact proof that our program of recovery and our work with the Steps are succeeding. It may very well need the discovery of a Progressive Power, and most certainly will require a progressive application of the Steps as well as a deepening of the inner work, which for many of us may include professional assistance. For the record, this is often where we discover other addictions, especially those involving relational or process addictions.

One final note is worth considering. We often hear that we need to surrender. Interestingly enough, that particular word cannot be found in the basic text of the Big Book of Alcoholics Anonymous. Given how often we hear of surrender, we must ask why it could be overlooked or omitted.

Perhaps it is because we do not actually surrender anything ... ever.

To surrender implies we are yielding something in which we still find value. And there is little evidence any of us give up something we still believe to have value for us. This may be why we often do hear someone say they surrender things and then take them back—over and over again. If we still value something, of course we would take it back.

However, the Big Book does talk of abandoning things. This is an important distinction. We only abandon something when it no longer has value to us. So perhaps this process of recovery in which we are engaged is in fact one of discovery that leads us to clarity that an addiction or a dysfunction does not serve us, that it does not have value. Thus we become willing to abandon it, and our work with the Twelve Steps and the Progressive Power then takes it from us.

One of the most powerful sections of the Big Book is the final page of the basic text. "Abandon yourself to God as you understand God." This is a direct connection back to Step Three. In Progressive Recovery we will find ourselves returning to it time and time again, always taking the next step toward greater abandoning of some aspect of self that no longer serves us.

A Toolkit for a Progressive Steps Two and Three

As described above, a progressive approach to a power greater than ourselves is going to ask us to work more deeply. We may need a Progressive Power, or we may need a progressive decision to turn our will and life over fueled by still greater willingness. Here are a few tools we recommend:

- Journaling or written inventory remains a valuable approach. Writing about what we believe with respect to a Higher Power, and what may make for a Progressive Power can be helpful. So too is writing that continues to convince us of the need for a larger solution, or to work more deeply.

- Discussing the state of one's belief as well as the state of one's recovery with another human being is priceless. It makes things more real for us. This is a role for a sponsor, a therapist, an advisor or a trusted friend.

- Many have found AA's *Came to Believe* to be very helpful as it targets Steps Two and Three.

- Quite a few have benefitted from *A Return to Love* by Marianne Williamson, which challenges us to look at a recovered state much differently.

- My book, *Seeing True: Ninety Contemplations in Ninety Days* is for some a useful workbook to explore beliefs about Higher Power.

Into Action with Steps Two and Three

In your journal, consider the following questions regarding Steps Two and Three. Once again, it is quite common for some of our efforts in this book to feel repetitive. There is powerful data that suggests our best approach for overcoming anything is to never stop trying. Please persist even if your work feels the same. Rest assured, it is never the same.

- Review your notes and thoughts related to Step One and the problem(s) you are facing. To what degree do you find yourself unable to believe that the situation can be addressed or removed? Have you lost faith in your program of recovery or the Twelve Steps? Are you unable to consider the possibility of things being made right with you? Tell yourself the truth.

- Does this suggest limitations in a Higher Power, or in your belief in a Higher Power? What would it take for you to believe? Or to be willing to believe? More importantly, what limitations do you see in your decision to turn your will and life (or if you prefer, your thoughts and your actions) over to a Progressive Power? In what ways do you find yourself unwilling?

- Make a list of friends, sponsors, advisors or other trusted people who have experience with Steps Two and Three, and the decision it asks of us. What guidance do they provide you? Have you questioned them about their ideas? Have you shared with them the limits of your own perspectives, beliefs or willingness? What evidence do you now have that will support you in deepening your Step Three decision?

- Do you know why you still cling? If not, what would you guess it is that causes a person like you to continue to hold onto something? What comfort, or pleasure, or satisfaction, or reassurance would it continue to hold? What would it take to abandon it? What would convince you?

Deepening the Connection to Power—Now

Step Eleven
Sought through prayer and meditation to improve
our conscious contact with God *as we understood
God*, praying only for knowledge of God's will
for us and the power to carry that out.

*Do you really think HP gives a damn if
you work the steps in order?*
—IRENE W.

*There's a whole lot of praying going on,
but not much listening.*
—PATRICK K.

There's a common statement heard in the rooms of recovery,
"The steps are listed in order, so you can work them in
order." While that may be initially useful, or at least orderly

and therefore useful guidance for those who are seeking comfort through structure, there is an entirely different way to consider Step Eleven.

If our problem is a lack of access to power, power that is greater than us, why wouldn't we deliberately seek to enhance the connection to power? After all, the Step does say we aim to improve conscious contact with power. And why wouldn't we add that effort sooner rather than later? Especially since we can anticipate some significant inner work coming in Steps Four through Nine where access to Progressive Power will serve us very well.

It is probably useful at this point to remind ourselves of the value of open minds. There is wide agreement that alcoholics and addicts often suffer from a certainty that is unfounded as well as an unwillingness to consider possibilities beyond our point of view. No place is this a more useful reminder than with Step Eleven. There are huge bodies of work and great experience from teachers and practitioners outside of recovery who are far more knowledgeable and experienced with spiritual practices than we are. It will serve us well to seek out their ideas, practices and knowledge.

Step Eleven points to two approaches: prayer and meditation. To be honest, many of us have ample experience with prayer either through past religious practice, use of prayers in the Big Book and other literature, or exposure to every imaginable kind of prayer used by friends and acquaintances both in recovery and beyond the rooms. Even atheists and agnostics use mantras or inspirational quotes in the same way a prayer might be used.

Perhaps it is simply a matter of finding prayers and practices which suit us well. However, there is one important point in the language of this step that is worth mentioning for our purposes.

Much of the praying that goes on in the rooms of recovery is self-serving or self-centered. That's hardly surprising, not because we are as selfish as we often hear, or that we often find ourselves in great personal troubles, but because in the end our only frame of reference is ourselves. Even when we pray for others, which is often encouraged as a way of breaking through self-centeredness, it is still being done in the service of our own spiritual development and well-being. We cannot not be self-interested.

Perhaps then we can seek for enlightened self-interest, to be more aware of our motivations even as we pray for others, or pray for knowledge of God's will for us and the power to carry it out. Perhaps we can stop bludgeoning ourselves with condemnation for being self-oriented, which is only human, and instead give thought to larger perspectives in which we can include our interests and well-being as part of spiritual practice. After all, the greater our growth and development, the greater the benefits to those around us. We ourselves are always a beneficiary of our own good work, while likewise benefitting others.

Assuming that prayer, or something inspirational or motivational can be adopted from others, or customized for your use, let's turn our attention to the subject of meditation.

Depending on our religious and faith-based experiences and history, we may have great biases about meditation. And yet, of all the disciplines that come to bear on the

Twelve Steps, none are richer than this. There are so many possibilities that perhaps the best way to proceed progressively is to offer some well-learned experience, then convey the many arenas in which we have found successes.

First, let's keep it very simple. One wise teacher said meditation is whatever happens while we're trying to meditate. Fortunately, that makes it possible for all of us to succeed despite our inner committee of critics. And rest assured, one aspect of recovery and healing is to leave behind the many senses of failure that many of us carry so heavily.

Another elder in recovery says we should find a form of meditation that works for us and practice as often as we are able. And no less a figure than Bill Wilson told us that when we failed or rebelled, we should simply resume when we were able.

It seems the wise and experienced folk are trying to give us permission to do the best we can. As one old timer said, "Damn it, my best is just going to have to be good enough. 'Cause I can't do it any better."

Having now created some open space for us to play and experiment with these ideas, but before we look at examples from which we can learn, what are the various purposes of meditation?

- Many of us have squirrels in our heads, and just like dogs in the park that love to chase them, they can distract us. At its most fundamental level, meditation can be used to settle the crazy thoughts, and even to bring us some inner peace and quiet.
- Beyond this quieting, many forms of meditation bring

us the opportunity to focus our attention and explorations to learn and understand better. When we advance in these arenas our spiritual recovery can advance as well.

- As silence becomes more common to our experience, many of us find that awareness and inspiration occur much more frequently. We can experience the intuition that the Big Book calls us to as a form of reliance.
- Some of us may encounter what has been called *the still, small voice* that can bring great comfort as well as clarity. Often our ability to observe ourselves grows as well, and as the Big Book promises, "We are in much less danger of excitement."
- In the end, meditation practice can open us up in the best of ways, including allowing us to become more patient, forgiving, compassionate and understanding.

Still, many of us find the prospect of meditation to be intimidating or frightening regardless of the potential benefits. We who are familiar with those challenges would suggest that you simply make an effort and see what might take root. Furthermore, you don't have to go it alone. Find a friend, or a group of people to share the experience. Over time it is likely to grow and deepen as layer upon layer opens to us.

Before we move into our experience with meditation, let's clarify one thing. While we don't wish to quibble, in its broadest sense meditation includes contemplation, contemplative prayer, mindfulness, and any number of other approaches. Our goal is not to categorize or protest any of them. Instead we want to explore them.

And there is one final thought that we have found to be quite comforting. Joel Goldsmith, who some call the greatest American mystic, said that the divine only needs an instant to restore and reawaken us. We need only make ourselves available, which seems wholly in keeping with the simplicity obviously espoused in the Twelve Steps of recovery. As a humorous aside, one drunk observed, "Well maybe HP only needs an instant, but I'm going to need a lot more time!"

A Toolkit for Progressive Step Eleven Meditation

Our experience, strength and hope suggest that one or more of these approaches will work for most anyone though you might have to experiment for some time to determine that. We'll start with those that are often found to be easier or more accessible, then progress toward those that may prove to be more difficult or require more practice. Once you begin in whatever way you begin, we would merely encourage you to keep experimenting, and try to increase and deepen your practice over time.

Twelve Step Meetings

There is no question that for many of us simply attending a recovery meeting is the easiest meditation, though it might be more accurate to call it contemplative meditation since we are typically trying to stay focused on a topic, or a step, or perhaps a speaker's story. For some of us, the most useful meetings are those that do have a strong focus because it helps us pay attention and thus to learn and grow more. If we can avoid the distractions of side conversations and cell phones, we are all the more likely to be present enough to get the most of the experience.

Working with Another Alcoholic (or Any Person)
Twelve Step programs model for us over and over and over again the importance of working with others, and especially the power of being present for others. As it says in the Big Book, in many instances nothing is more effective at keeping us sober than working with another alcoholic. At a minimum, if we are able to listen attentively, we will often find ourselves able to stay fully present for surprisingly long periods of time. Think of this as a practice of centering meditation that brings us into the moment.

Journaling, Written Inventory and Study
Whether we call it journaling, written inventory, or even study, when we delve into literature with pencil, pad and highlighter, it is in fact a focusing activity that qualifies as meditation. Largely, this is a simple means of paying close attention to the exclusion of distractions. It can be practiced anywhere, including as part of morning routines or as part of our final reflections on a day. We also recommend it as a tool for note-taking during Twelve Step meetings. And of course, the ability to stop at any time during the course of the affairs of the day to take stock is not only true to Step Ten, which we'll discuss later, but a powerful reflective practice.

Conversation and Dialogue
Since the recovering community is a very talkative one, why not consider effective conversation and dialogue to be

meditation? After all, effective interaction with others can be very fruitful when it aids us in understanding. That latter point deserves a little clarification. There are any number of forms of talking which are not especially useful because they can be mindless, distracting or even defensive. That is not to say that small talk has no value, rather to acknowledge that talking for social purposes should not be considered the same as focused conversation. Indeed, the Big Book actually says that "a message that can interest and hold these alcoholic people must have depth and weight."

Mindfulness

This is a practice which is much in fashion in recent years. Any search online or in a bookstore will find a very large number of options. Generally, mindfulness lends itself to formal practices of which there are likewise a wide variety. All in all, these practices seek to bring one's attention into the present moment. This is often accomplished through use of the breath or focusing approaches that give a focal point for one's attention and awareness.

Walking Meditation

In his writing, Bill Wilson acknowledged that sometimes when he was the most disturbed, he would simply go for a walk and count his steps. Many recovering people find walking and hiking to be deeply grounding. If you wish, there are more formal practices that are used in various settings including Buddhism, Zen, and contemplative spirituality settings.

Study or Meditation with Groups

There are an endless number of groups of people who meet to study, pray and meditate together. Find one that focuses in a way that suits you and make a commitment to it. Your involvement can be as short or long as you wish, just remember that staying focused has inherent benefits, so something longer than short-term involvement will likely be beneficial.

Guided Meditations

For those who need something to direct them, guided meditations can be the perfect solution. These can range from simple words to visualizations, and may include chanting or singing. There are even candle gazing and other focusing approaches geared to support us with something to guide us. Even laughter meditations can be beneficial. They can be found as recordings, online or in person.

Embodiment Practices

Many of us benefit from being brought into our bodies because we can be so distracted by our thoughts. Sometimes this can be as simple as an art or craft that brings us into the moment. Bodywork such as massage can likewise bring us to the present experience. So too do martial and Eastern arts like tai chi. Yoga has become so commonplace and beneficial that it is now widely accessible in an incredible range of approaches.

Resources

Here are a few of the resources we've found to be useful for those in recovery:

- Christian contemplative practices including Father Richard Rohr and his book, *Breathing Under Water*, which is based on the Twelve Steps,
- New Thought approaches such as Joel Goldsmith's *The Art of Meditation*,
- Buddhist orientations including Kevin Griffin's *One Breath at a Time*, Thérèse Jacobs-Stewart's *Mindfulness and the 12 Steps*, and Eric Rainbeau's *Basic Sobriety*,
- Eckhart Tolle's *The Power of Now*, and
- My audio set, *Breathing, Releasing and Breaking Through*

A Final Thought

One day in a recovery meeting on meditation those with some time in recovery were very philosophical about their practices. A guy who was relatively new in the rooms was asked to share. He sheepishly admitted that the only thing that quieted his mind was waxing his car. One of the old timers replied: "Then waxing your car is a good meditation for you."

Into Action with Step Eleven

In your journal, consider the following questions regarding Step Eleven:

- Before beginning contemplative practices of prayer or meditation, what biases do you have either for or against such practice(s)? Why do you seem to be resistant? Can you find it within yourself to be willing to set aside your closed mindedness? What can you do to support your willingness?

- Select one or two of the suggested forms of meditation or books in the toolkit above. Which did you choose and why? Was your choice influenced by the previous question about willingness?
- What pre-planning or support from others would be useful to encourage your follow through: setting a time of day, finding a partner to share the experience, seeking out a class or other practice space, discussing it with your sponsor or spiritual advisor, or collecting more information? To what lengths are you willing to go?
- What do you experience with the practice(s)? Did you gain any insights? Discover any other factors that facilitate or hinder your practice(s)?

Fact Finding and Truth Telling

Step Four
Made a searching and fearless moral inventory of ourselves.

Step Five
Admitted to God, to ourselves, and to another
human being the exact nature of our wrongs.

*Many of us have tried to hold onto our old ideas, and
the result was nil until we let go absolutely.*
—ALCOHOLICS ANONYMOUS

*Invariably we find that at some time in the past we have
made decisions based on self which have placed us in a
position to be harmed.*
—ALCOHOLICS ANONYMOUS

It is with personal inventory that Progressive Recovery makes a
significant departure from the traditional view of the Twelve

Steps. We do so with good reason.

Let's revisit a primary purpose for Progressive Recovery. It is our experience that a number of us who practice good programs of recovery arrive at a point where progress seems blocked. Typically, there is something intractable that simply is not yielding to the steps as we are practicing them. Or we reach a point of low-grade complacency or discouragement despite our step work. Too often we find ourselves among others who merely normalize our situation. "Remember, it's one day at a time." "Just don't drink today." "Maybe you should talk to a newcomer." "Those are some first-world problems you have."

The point is not to criticize the rooms of recovery or the people in them, but to understand that the purpose of the Twelve Steps is to reveal over and over again each next layer of blockage to power. If we are making progress, we should be discovering deeper aspects of ourselves that limit and hinder us in our recovery. We need to see that getting stuck is normal, and merely a sign of the need to increase the depth of our recovery efforts via the Steps.

That said, we often hear that it is difficult to admit to challenges in recovery. Our great fear is that you, just like many others, will be unable to see or admit that you have become stuck. As we mentioned before, our experience tells us there are two conclusions we might reach at such crucial moments in recovery. Possibly we will decide that the Twelve Steps are not sufficient to solve more fundamental problems within us. Or we might determine we are too flawed or broken for the Steps to restore us.

Please be as resolved as possible, and more fearless and

more thorough than you thought you could be. Let us reassure you we have found that the principles of the Steps will always be successful in restoring us to the degree we are able to work them more deeply, which sometimes requires different approaches and supports.

What are these advanced principles of fact-finding and truth-telling as they are reflected in Progressive Steps Four and Five?

First, here's a quick reframe of these steps. The Fourth Step states we're going to make a fearless and searching moral inventory. And the Fifth says further that we're going to tell ourselves, the Progressive Power and another human being all about it.

Let's start with the facts—and nothing but the facts—by looking differently at this idea of a moral inventory. While we may have begun by looking at our behaviors and our morals, a Progressive Inventory is not about morality but seeks to become increasingly nonjudgmental. While blaming others will never produce a solution, self-condemnation is devastatingly damaging to our recovery since it merely increases our sense of guilt or shame. Guilt is the product of finding fault with our actions; shame comes from believing we are fundamentally flawed.

We've heard it said that shame and guilt can make us thirsty—for alcohol, or something. It is not uncommon for people solidly in recovery to find their way back to their addiction or to a new one because of unresolved guilt or shame. And once someone slips in their recovery, the downward spiral can be unrelenting. We may never see them again, or they may never again find recovery.

There is an interesting twist in the language of the Big Book. It does not say we are looking for what is bad or wrong in order to turn it into that which is good or right. It also does not tell us we are sick trying to get well. Instead it proposes we are seeking to discover what blocks us off from Higher Power. Then it proposes we are to look for causes and conditions which block us off from the power.

Of course! If lack of power is our problem, and there is power available, we are asked to examine through personal inventory what blocks power from flowing. The purpose of the Steps is not self-improvement, nor is it behavioral modification, rather it is restoration of power and through that to experience a restoration of sanity. That is not to say that efforts to improve ourselves or our behavior are to be shunned, rather to understand that is not the point and purpose of the Steps, which aim toward more fundamental matters.

Then we find two key phrases often repeated though not always well understood.

- "Many of us have tried to hold onto our old ideas and the result was nil until we let go absolutely."
- "Invariably we find that at some time in the past we have made decisions based on self which have placed us in a position to be harmed."

Progressive Recovery uses personal inventory to examine our underlying beliefs and perceptions, some of which run quite deeply within us.

Let's look at a fairly common example to explain this

approach, after which we'll explore the means by which such an inventory can be conducted.

Consider Jennifer. She's long-time sober, works the Twelve Steps on an ongoing basis, talks regularly to her sponsor, actively sponsors several women, involves herself in her home group, and attends several meetings a week. Jennifer has also had trouble with relationships with men. Granted they are much improved as a result of recovery, but they are still far from functional or fulfilling. She just can't seem to find the right guy—in the rooms of recovery or outside them.

While Jennifer has included all the broken relationships in her life in her previous inventories, she's never really explored her earliest experiences with men, those that include her birth father and two stepfathers. None of them were bad men, though addiction was involved in some cases. However, they were all emotionally unavailable to Jennifer, either because of addiction or simply a lack of emotional capacities.

With deeper exploration via a personal inventory with her sponsor as well as professional therapy, Jennifer discovers that as a child she came to believe that men were simply unavailable, that they would neglect or ignore her needs. She also realized that in her heart, she believed she was somehow unlovable, which to a child fully explains the unavailability of these men. Worse still, she determined that the only way to get their attention was to do things for them, which as she grew older came to include taking care of their needs in exchange for their attention.

With this lens, she could see that she repeatedly had

found her way to men who were simply unavailable. With few exceptions she would try to win their affections by providing for them in any number of ways, including being the primary breadwinner, a caretaker for their emotional and physical needs, and of course, a sex partner. Invariably the relationships proved to be unsustainable.

Let's now put Jennifer's experience in the context of the Big Book's four-column inventory with a little bit of Progressive Recovery embellishment. At the end of the chapter we'll present a fuller version of that approach to inventory.

- Column 1—Who or what do we have a grievance against, or a problem?
  » Jennifer: A man in particular or men in general.
- Column 2—What happened, i.e., what's the story behind it?
  » Jennifer: The backstory as described above, i.e., unavailable men and her need to take care of them and their needs.
- Column 3—How does it affect us? What's the emotional impact?
  » Jennifer: Frustration, discouragement, lack of fulfillment.
- Column 4—What have we brought to this situation? What old ideas or decisions based on self are involved?
  » Jennifer:
    › A belief that men are unavailable.
    › An old idea that she is unlovable.
    › A decision that she must do something for men to gain and hold their attention.

- Note: In cases such as fear or lack of fulfillment, where there are not obvious items for Column 1 or 2, simply start with Column 3.

Jennifer is unable to engage in a satisfying relationship with a man. She lacks the power to find a guy with whom she is well-suited, and she has demonstrated no ability to sustain such a relationship if she found one. She is blocked off by the beliefs, old ideas and decisions based on self.

At this point, it is useful to notice that the Big Book uses a particular idea that is worth examining. It describes two kinds of alcoholic, one that is "more demanding" and one that is "more gracious." The former is often described as the part of some alcoholics' personalities which is "being an asshole." In contrast, Jennifer has never acted that way, instead she self-compromises by what is often described as people-pleasing behavior. This makes for a remarkably different inventory—rather than looking for "bad" behavior that injures others, one must look for "good" behavior that injures oneself, while simultaneously injuring others. Of course, each of us has some mix of both within us, though most seem to lean significantly in one direction or the other.

That said, we can readily demonstrate varying themes within any person. We can also look more deeply into all our behavioral or emotional challenges. As it turns out, many of our behaviors and the patterns that underlie our lives are symptomatic of underlying beliefs, old ideas and decisions based on self. However, many of us have never looked thoroughly enough via personal inventory to understand ourselves. And far too many of us have rejected the idea of professional assistance even though it is strongly recommended in the Big Book.

Note that the particulars of any one person's underlying psychology, while comparable to those of others, are always unique to that individual's experience. While we can learn from the understanding others gain, their exact story will never quite fit ours. We often hear our problems in recovery are not unique, which is certainly true in a general sense, but it turns out our personal experience is always unique to us. Thus, our recovery work must have unique aspects as well.

Let's be clear that it is quite common for our initial inventories in recovery to reflect less depth. And that's a perfectly good way to gain recovery. Start with issues and concerns that are obvious, clean them up in every way one can via the Twelve Steps, but don't stop there. Work more deeply over time in a sustained way with personal inventory. It is our experience that recovery will always reveal still more opportunity to deepen our understanding.

Sometimes we will hear that one need only do a single personal inventory. If that suffices to move one into a steady and growing spiritual recovery, or at least enduring sobriety, we find no disagreement. However, for many of us there will necessarily be a long and steady process of Steps Four and Five over time. Said Patrick K., an elder in recovery, "Anytime you have a major change in your life, especially if it is an upset, it's probably time for another personal inventory. Regardless, one a year is a good practice to continue your growth."

A Toolkit for a Progressive Steps Four and Five

There are many resources available for personal inventory. And for each of them you'll find advocates, some of whom will insist their preferred approach is the best one. While we're happy to support anyone's perspective, our experience tells us that the nature and sensitivity of these steps is such that we recommend you experiment with tools and approaches until you find one that works well for you. This can include simply adopting the one recommended by your Twelve Step program or using approaches your sponsor has found helpful.

However, we do know that Progressive Recovery is more likely to produce benefit to the degree that one moves beyond behaviors and symptoms toward underlying causes and conditions. Likewise, we are confident that professional help can be very useful in deepening one's recovery.

Assets or Strengths Inventory

It is not uncommon for our negativity about ourselves to be so strong that we further injure ourselves inadvertently as a result of personal inventory. That is an unfortunate byproduct of our attempts to look within ourselves through the old negative ideas we so often have about ourselves.

One useful strategy is to include character assets or a strengths inventory. Some of those who have practiced deeply with personal inventory would say that in fact every so-called character defect has a character asset side to it. We fully endorse that idea. At a minimum, looking at our strengths provides a helpful contrast. At best, looking honestly at our positive attributes creates access to emotional sobriety because all of us truly are doing the best we are able using the best character traits available to us in any given moment. As we have heard it said, "At any moment, what I am doing really is the best I have access to based on the time, place, circumstances and old ideas currently existing within me."

We've added a column to weave in strengths and assets to counterbalance the inventory at this point. In the following chapter, we'll introduce still more of this idea.

An Afterword on Trauma and Growth

Often, we find the underlying causes and conditions are highly sensitized by the presence of traumas in our lives, especially as children or through violence. We've also learned that trauma can result from frequent incidence of low-intensity stressors such as abandonment, betrayal, abuse or neglect.[2]

This is an extremely important point because stress and trauma are experiential. They often are not readily accessible through written inventory. Indeed, many of our psychological adaptations serve to wall off and buffer us from such wounds.

We strongly recommend therapeutic support, especially from those trained in dealing with trauma. This is true for many of us even when overt signs of trauma are not apparent. The section entitled On Trauma and Growth, which follows our exploration of the Steps, provides more information.

Into Action with Steps Four and Five

In your journal, consider the following questions regarding Steps Four and Five.

The following format can assist with getting to causes and conditions for a Progressive Recovery Step Four. Remember, this is not about who you are, but about your beliefs, many of which are unconscious, old ideas, which are not so easily seen or understood, and decisions made based on self—often from a subconscious level in order to survive as a child.

Write out Step Four as follows: (See chart at the end of this chapter.)

- With whom or what do I have an issue, resentment or annoyance? This can be a person, institution, situation or life itself.
- What happened, i.e., what is the "story"? Be reasonably brief.
- How does it affect me? Describe the feelings. Where do you feel them in the body? What do they feel like? Have you felt these feelings on other occasions? What is the emotional impact? Do you feel ashamed? Try not to minimize what you feel, or to explain away the feeling.
- Breathe into the feelings. Feel them, then let them go. Do not stay too long in the feelings. Any insights?
- What have I brought to this situation? Does this remind me of other situations that feel the same? What old ideas or decisions based on self are involved? Are there beliefs I have about this situation, or about myself?

Look beyond the behavior. Feel free to ask yourself what causes the behavior.

- What are some of my character assets or something positive about this activity? How have I been able to use these feelings, or the underlying things I bring to it, to benefit myself or others? Once again, do not minimize yourself or your value.

Practice Step Five as follows:

- Share what you have found with your sponsor, a trusted friend, therapist or clergyman. What have you discovered while sharing? What changed in your perspective about the situation or yourself?
- What are the things I can do to nurture and take care of myself?

A Five Column Example of Step Four

With whom or what do I have an issue, resentment or annoyance? This can be a person, institution, situation or life itself.	What happened? What's the story behind it? Be as brief as you are able while still being descriptive enough.	How does it affect me? What is the emotional impact? Where in the body do I feel these feelings? How would I describe the feelings to someone else? Do I have shame about myself? Try not to minimize what you feel, or to explain away the feeling. Breathe into the feelings for self-care.	What have I brought to this situation? Does this remind me of other situations that feel the same? What old ideas or decisions based on self are involved? Are there beliefs I have about this situation, or about myself? Look beyond the behavior. Feel free to ask yourself what causes the behavior.	What are some of my character assets or something positive about this activity? How have I been able to use these feelings, or the underlying things I bring to it, to benefit myself or others? Once again, do not minimize yourself or your value.

Clearing the Channel

Step Six
Were entirely ready to have God remove
all these defects of character.

Step Seven
Humbly asked God to remove our shortcomings.

৯ঌ

*"Higher Power changes men and women on the inside,
then works through them in changing the outside."*
—BROTHER G DAWG

৯ঌ

In Steps Four and Five we were quite clear about the need to move toward underlying causes and conditions that produce the behaviors and attitudes that have resulted in so much difficulty, even in recovery. And the Big Book states that the byproduct of that personal inventory effort will be that we "swallow some large chunks of truth about ourselves." From our perspective, the deepening of the inventory makes this statement all the more accurate. As we begin to see and understand the underlying patterns in our lives it can become overwhelming. When we begin to break through the denial and delusion many of us unconsciously used to maintain our unexamined lives, it can be simultaneously quite disturbing and very exhilarating.

We believe that Steps Six and Seven are the lynchpin in Progressive Recovery. It is where our attention turns toward solutions—solutions for large, enduring or lifelong difficulties. It is important to reframe some language in these two steps that many find to be potentially problematic in advancing our recovery.

Given that our personal inventory will increasingly uncover beliefs, old ideas and decisions based on self that have been unconscious, and that we are learning the destructiveness of guilt and shame as they affect our recovery, many of us must find a different orientation to what are called "defects of character" and "shortcomings."

We do not fault those who arrived at that language so many years ago. And no doubt, many of the deeds and misdeeds of alcoholics and addicts warrant stern perspectives and language. Yet we are increasingly convinced that the root causes of our addictions, our attitudes and our behaviors are in the realm of false perceptions and misunderstandings about ourselves, other people, our lives and the world.

Some will protest what they see to be the undue softening of such an approach. We understand the concern. And we also understand that the long-term effect of punitive perspectives is ultimately not helpful in Progressive Recovery. Yes, we are fully responsible for our actions and perspectives;

at the same time, in truth, we are typically innocent of malice or wrongful intent. As one wise elder said, "I didn't ever wake up in the morning planning to harm others or myself. No doubt I did harm, but on some deeper level I had no idea what was going on. I was asleep at the wheel."

Perhaps it is better to simply refer to character defects as causes and conditions, or old ideas and decisions based on self. Doing so cements the idea that until we somehow release these misperceptions and false understandings, they will continue to be corrosive in our lives. At worst, they will drive us from our recovery back into addiction.

Another important point will be seeing that the challenges we now face in this arena are beyond mere self-improvement. Sometimes we demonstrate an ability to change our behaviors, though in the realm of so called process addictions like food and eating disorders, relationship addictions, and financial or gambling compulsions it is often yet one more level of powerlessness. Whether or not we can alter a behavior, what are we to do with intractable matters, or in changing a belief that we hold to be true? It's not as if we can simply stop believing it. And where our old ideas apply to our very nature or our identity, it becomes increasingly clear we will need spiritual aid in letting go.

Because the means of letting go of old ideas is beyond our present ability, and can only be addressed by some Progressive Power, this idea of asking for help is all the more important. We are not looking for behavioral or attitudinal improvement, but more fundamental alterations within our being.

Let's first begin by affirming the importance of clarity about the nature of the problem. Asking for support in the removal of a symptom is just about as effective as hoping that by reducing a fever we will somehow be cured of the underlying bacteria or virus that is the cause. Asking for help for a behavioral improvement is only a starting point; we must ask for assistance with the underlying old ideas, the causes and conditions, or the decisions based on self.

And we must become willing to seek out and accept assistance as we can find it anywhere in the larger world. Many of us continue to hold onto ideas of self-sufficiency, which is antithetical to the idea of a Progressive Power. Or we seek to control the terms of the assistance that may come to us. We must be willing to go to any lengths to discover the information, approaches or expertise that we may need. If this takes us beyond the rooms of recovery, we need to be fully supported in the rooms for those decisions.

Sometimes we find we are forced to let go of some of the relationships in recovery that are holding us back. Remember, as we delve more deeply and ask discomforting questions, it may prove to be just as uncomfortable for others as it is for us. As a result, and without malice, they may steer us clear of the important inner work that is being revealed. A great master once said that the sign of a strong spiritual path is the revelation of new aspects of healing that are asked of us. Finding more challenges in recovery is not a sign of a weak program, but an indicator that the Twelve Steps are working at depth to restore us.

Many of us experience difficulty looking more deeply at ourselves or are resistant to receiving information or assistance beyond the rooms. One prayer we have found useful as a powerful statement of willingness is as follows:

Please take from me whatever needs to be removed
so I can move forward. If it can't be removed, please
change it within me in any way necessary. Help me
to see what I need to see, feel what I need to feel, and
learn what I need to learn. Help me to be willing.

Sometimes we can complement this powerful prayer with
another simple one:

Please show me the nature of my unwillingness so I
can pray for its release.

One observation we've made as we work the Twelve Steps
more deeply is that Progressive Power does not seem able to
remove anything we cannot see or acknowledge. Our cur-
rent state of understanding necessarily honors our oldest
and deepest ideas until the moment that we can own them
within ourselves and become willing to relinquish them.
Sometimes that process requires pain and suffering. However, we do not subscribe to the idea that pain is inevitable,
nor do we think for a moment that suffering is optional. We
see from our experience that we must experience whatever
it is we must in order to become convinced of the hopelessness and futility of our path and our ways.

As noted earlier, it is interesting to discover the Big Book
does not once mention the word "surrender," though it is
certainly a common one in the recovery community. Upon
reflection, and again based on our experience, we observe
that we do not seem to surrender anything as long as we
cannot see it clearly or for as long as we continue to see value

in it. Instead, and this may be why the Big Book used the word abandon, we suspect that until we are fully ready to release something, it will not be taken from us, or altered in any significant way.

This point is worth a short explanation. As long as we value something, we do not and cannot release it. The inventory work and the repetitive application of these efforts at Steps Six and Seven aid us in reevaluating things. When we finally see clearly and no longer value the beliefs, old ideas, causes and conditions, or decisions based on self, then it is possible to abandon them, to let them go because we no longer desire them.

Rather than punishing ourselves for our failure to progress with some intractable challenge, we have found great value in gentleness and self-forgiveness. We have come to see that we are simply stuck, most often unconsciously. And when finally the nature of our inner obstructions are fully revealed, most of us prove to be excellent students and highly cooperative.

During these efforts to discover and release our old ideas, the causes and conditions, and decisions based on self, we often see that we can become quite discouraged. We certainly recommend the basic ideas of service and working with others as an ongoing remedy.

As we introduced in the previous chapter, there may be great value in taking on a positive and optimistic approach to the process of letting go. Since many of us have old hypercritical ideas about ourselves, many of us find great value in an assets inventory. When taken with a sponsor, a spiritual advisor, a good friend, a minister, or a therapist, an assets inventory can be very beneficial to see the great amount of good that resides within us. At a minimum it will remind us that while we may be struggling, we are fundamentally decent women and men looking in every way we are able to get out from under our difficulties.

As we mentioned in the last chapter, it is inevitable that every character defect has a reverse side to it. It is this contrast and the opportunity to see ourselves in a new light that interests us. Here are some examples we have found to be common:

- The need to control is invariably tied to some kind of self-protection. That need for safety may stem from misperception, but self-care is critically important. When we label ourselves a "control freak," to be fair and honest we may also want to admit that it is simultaneously an effort to take care of ourselves.
- Some of us have been ridiculed for over-thinking. No doubt, that can be a real challenge to our sobriety as well as driving others away from us. At the same time, being able to think deeply and richly is a great gift. Perhaps the issue is not the thinking, but the lack of discipline. Why not consider it an asset and set about to learn how to use it effectively?
- Sometimes one person's stubbornness is another person's patience. Or hard-headedness can easily be reframed as persistence. The value is in the eye of the beholder.
- In a reverse example, many of us are acknowledged for our responsibility, it is seen as a strength. In the right circumstances, it is valuable. At the same time, feeling

responsible for others can be terribly codependent and damaging to ourselves and others.

The larger point is that most all of us are fundamentally people of good will. The Buddhists would even remind us that our essential nature is "basic goodness." This seems akin to the great ideas in the Big Book that tell us the fundamental idea of God will be found deep within every man, woman and child, though it may be obscured by any number of challenges.

Some of us find that as we go about the channel clearing of Step Six and Seven it is quite helpful to deliberately engage in regular exposure to anything that lifts our spirits. For some it is art, for others great food, or a good movie. At a minimum, this can restore some balance to our self-perception. At best, it may just provide a Progressive Power with enough of an opening deep within us so that we can be remade in some important ways.

We also have found that self-care is extraordinarily useful and important. While some traditionalists will say we are being selfish or self-centered in focusing on our own needs, we have learned through painful efforts over time that self-nurturance is an important part of healing and growing. We know you can't give away what you don't have. How could we possibly seek to be of service and benefit to others without rendering the same to ourselves? How can we offer love without first being loving?

We have concluded that service, assets or strengths inventory, and self-care can coexist quite well together. Indeed, it might be they are designed to work together.

It can be useful to remember a few things while undertaking Steps Six and Seven. First, a long period of reconstruction lies ahead. We do not change by leaps and bounds, rather by fits and starts with occasional quantum leaps that too often slip away. Progress is a curious and uneven matter. Regardless, the effort we invest is one thing at which we can succeed.

Failure is not failure. It is part of the process that leads to success. And we must try to remember that the very nature of the spiritual path is for more to be revealed in terms of what blocks us off from power. There is always one more inner blockage to be addressed, and yet progress, healing and restoration are progressive.

Years ago, an AA speaker stated that the point and purpose of recovery is to awaken more and more over time, and especially to remember that we cannot solve self-sufficiency with still more self-reliance. Instead, we move to release self-centered approaches. After all, if self could solve the problems of self, there would be no need for Twelve Steps or a Progressive Power.

One final word from our experience and from an earlier reference. It does not seem to matter what we believe about Progressive Power. You can never believe in any moment any more than what you believe. Thankfully, Progressive Power is above our opinion of it. The key is not actually a focus on Progressive Power, but on our ability to relinquish believing that we are our own power, and thereby letting go of self-sufficiency and self-reliance.

Wisdom tells us to start where you are. It will be good enough.

A Toolkit for a Progressive Step Six and Seven

We have found that this is an arena in which it can be more challenging to find tools and approaches. Nevertheless, here are a few ideas:

- Journaling is a powerful monitoring tool. Whether used as formal inventory or merely taking stock, we recommend it without limit.
- Meditation can be such a powerful tool for insight and awareness. We encourage you to explore this arena as earlier proposed.
- *Drop the Rock—Removing Character Defects—Steps Six and Seven*, by Todd W. and Sara S., has been used by many to great effect.
- Al-Anon's *Blueprints for Progress* inventory booklet can be remarkably useful in helping with asset inventory. While it does explore our so-called character defects, it balances nicely with positive self-appraisal.
- Many of us have had great positive self-assessments through a commercial product, *StrengthsFinder 2.0*. It is a well-researched approach that establishes what some call their sweet spot, which is very useful in gaining accurate self-appraisal.
- Another resource many have embraced is the book *What's In the Way Is the Way* by Mary O'Malley. It can be very useful in reframing how we view the difficulties we encounter within ourselves.

Into Action with Steps Six and Seven

To work more deeply with these steps, the following prayers can be used. If you prefer a different approach, any prayer that addresses false beliefs, underlying conditions, or our attitudes can be effective. We are asking for fundamental changes within our being, not just behavioral improvement. Remember when the causes and conditions are altered, behaviors invariably change because they are based on our old ideas. In addition, language matters. If the notion of "character defects" or "shortcomings" is shame-producing, consider setting them aside and embracing language that is reflective of new ideas and ways of being.

> Please take from me whatever needs to be removed
> so I can move forward. If it can't be removed, please
> change it within me in any way necessary. Help me
> to see what I need to see, feel what I need to feel, and
> learn what I need to learn. Help me to be willing.

Sometimes if we still feel stuck, we can complement this powerful prayer with another one:

> Please show me the nature of my unwillingness so I
> can pray for its release and work with releasing
> practices.

By all means, use the power of meditation and silence as a tool for listening for guidance. Refer to Step Eleven for forms of meditation that may be useful to you. And always keep your journal close at hand. When guidance comes, we find it very useful to capture it in writing since it can so easily slip away in the same way that dreams vanish if we do not capture them.

The previous quote in this chapter "… we are increasingly convinced that the root causes of our addictions, our attitudes and our behaviors, are in the realm of false perceptions and misunderstandings about ourselves, other people, our lives and the world…" provides fodder for further investigation.

- What underlying old ideas, causes, conditions or decisions based on self need to be removed or changed within me so that I can move forward? How do these relate to the outcomes in my life that are so problematic?
- In addition to prayer and meditation, what practices can I use to support releasing old ideas and decisions based on self? Therapeutic or spiritual advisors? Workshops or retreats? Forgiveness practices?

Living the Amended Life

Step Eight
Made a list of all persons we had harmed and
became willing to make amends to them all.

Step Nine
Made direct amends whenever possible, except
when to do so would injure them or others.

*"I did then what I knew how to do.
Now that I know better, I do better."*
—MAYA ANGELOU

Maya Angelou's perspective is a fine place to begin when
thinking about amends. It acknowledges that for many of
us much of what we feel guilty about manifested from nothing more than our own ignorance. Often, we do not understand ourselves and what drives us, and sometimes we do
not clearly see our effect on others. Yet as our awareness and

understanding grows, the way in which we see ourselves and our world is altered in extraordinary ways.

Let's talk about our growing awareness of the consequences of our alcoholism or addiction. And let's do so through this lens provided in the opening quote by Maya Angelou.

Most of us arrived at recovery thinking we were bad, and that if we could just become good our problems would be alleviated, or at least mitigated. So many of our earliest amends involved apologies and behavioral improvement. Of course, with the removal of alcohol and drugs, some improvements are readily attained.

Later we began to understand we have been quite sick, that addiction is a disease, not a matter of morals. This put important context around amends as we began to see our mistakes in a much different light. We still had things that needed to be made right, but increasingly the amends were through our healing. As we left more and more of the sickness of addiction behind, much of the fruit of the healing showed up in our lives, our behavior and our relationships. Very likely any number of those early "shortcomings" such as dishonesty, stealing and the like begin to fade away.

As our understanding grows still further in Progressive Recovery, as we gain awareness that the roots of our maladies are within us in the form of old ideas and decisions based on self, and as those begin to shift with our Step Seven efforts, we will certainly see still more improvement in behaviors and attitudes.

One wise woman reminds us that to amend something is for it to change. First, we see this in behavior and attitudes, but later the change is reflected in our personalities, our lives and our very being. Over time the purpose of the Twelve Steps is to reawaken us and to lead us increasingly toward our potential, to leave behind the damaged, sick and broken person we believed ourselves to be.

Let's begin by framing the nature of Progressive Amends by considering how things are made right with others, with ourselves, with a Progressive Power, and ultimately with life itself.

Every outer behavior or attitude is a reflection of an inner state. As our inner state is repaired, or amended, through the application of the Steps, the ways we act and present ourselves necessarily change. As we progress, many of us begin to practice living amends. For example, someone who has a history of stealing money may become very generous, consistently leaving large tips to servers, making anonymous contributions, offering their time and services free to others in the world, or becoming financially charitable. Or someone who came to understand how neglectful they were of others might become quite reliable in showing up for others, or look for ways of recognizing others. In short, the way we live our lives becomes the opposite of our failings.

Further still is the notion of living the amended life— where we live in ways that are entirely at odds with our old ideas. For example: someone who believed they were worthless becomes a successful businessman or woman, making economic contributions in their community. Or another who was an atheist becomes a minister. Or yet another who discovered they were in fact misgendered, transitioned from female to male, and then found a career helping others in similar situations.

The point is not that our behavior improves, rather that we become entirely different people, living more truly to ourselves and our souls. Often, we find that the intuition the Big Book promises as a result of the Twelve Steps begins to govern our lives in remarkable and unpredictable ways. To thine own self be true becomes the amended life, and through living that amended life, the lives of others are benefited. Service becomes the fruit of our recovery rather than an effort we make to do and be better.

Let's return to Jennifer's story from the chapter on Steps Four and Five. If you recall, she is long-time sober but has a troubling and unfulfilling history in her relationships with men, dating all the way back to the unavailable adult men in her life when she was a child. Here again is her inventory in this arena:

- Column 1—Who or what do we have a grievance against, or a problem?
  » Jennifer: A man in particular or men in general.
- Column 2—What happened, i.e., what's the story behind it?
  » Jennifer: The backstory as described above, i.e., unavailable men and her need to take care of them and their needs.
- Column 3—How does it affect us? What's the emotional impact?
  » Jennifer: Frustration, discouragement, lack of fulfillment.

- Column 4—What have we brought to this situation? What old ideas or decisions based on self are involved?
  » Jennifer:
  › A belief that men are unavailable.
  › An old idea that she is unlovable.
  › A decision that she must do something for men to gain and hold their attention.

While Jennifer works in her recovery with her therapist, sponsor and spiritual advisor to improve her interactions with men, she practices a continuing Step Seven, asking her Progressive Power to address her underlying beliefs. At each encounter with a man, she seeks to remember that men can be available, that she is lovable, and that she need not earn their appreciation. At the same time, she refrains from attempts to gain their approval, their attention or their love. She is practicing behavioral amends, as well as laying down a path of living amends.

To be healed in this regard, Jennifer has engaged in some difficult healing work with her therapist. As part of that inner work, she must also return to her mother and step-fathers to learn more and to make those relationships right. As she begins to date men, she must learn to watch for all the signs she formerly ignored.

Eventually her Progressive Recovery and amends work will lead her to meet men who are available and nurturing. At this point she must battle her tendencies to try to earn their continued attentions. And she begins a continuing written inventory of all the ways the voices in her head tell her she is unworthy.

At some point, Jennifer finds a man with whom she can engage in a committed and healthy relationship. It becomes a place in which she can practice amended living, including teaching her children what she has learned, working with others in recovery who have similar needs, and even volunteering in domestic violence shelters. All of this reinforces the deep healing of old ideas and decisions based on self. She is increasingly living the amended life.

It is here we realize that in order to give things away, we must learn them for ourselves and come to embody them. Then, we can offer them to others. At this point we have been remade by the principles within the Twelve Steps.

And still our inner work is not done. There is always a new layer of healing that will be revealed with continued practice. Our recovery and the realization of our potential becomes progressive, which allows for a progressive realization of the benefits that come in recovery.

We have moved far beyond improved behavior and attitudes. We have literally been remade. Power is flowing in remarkable ways because the blockages within us have been addressed with the application of the steps.

Let's take a moment to reframe what is an all-too-common experience for many of us when we find ourselves stuck. We refer to the times when we are simply unable to live in an amended way. We can't get out from under our old habits. Remember, there are no failures, only more information to aid us in deepening our Step Four inventory, advancing our Step Seven practices, and slowly being remade by Progressive Power.

One of the revelations that will come to us as we work

more deeply with living the amended life will be in learning that self-willing our way into greater recovery is not possible. Self-willed efforts will reveal that self-will is not the solution, but the problem. And the difficulties that come from that self-will become that which can teach us. Especially when the frustrations of failing take us back over and over again into Steps Four, Five, Six and Seven.

Just for a moment, let's digress to an old biblical adage—that you can't pour new wine into old wineskins. Of course, it is ironic that ancient wisdom involving alcohol can be a teaching tool for alcoholics, or anyone else for that matter.

What this adage teaches is that we cannot force new ideas or new ways of being into ourselves without making room by discarding the old ones. Trying to self-will our way into being better selves will create stress. That stress is useful for further step work to understand what still blocks us off from power. Remember, we're told that as long as we hold onto old ideas, we cannot make progress.

Here again is the secret within the Steps. We are without access to power to remake ourselves and our behaviors. Using inventory to find what blocks us off from Progressive Power, we look deeper and deeper and deeper for underlying causes and conditions. We ask Progressive Power for help. We ask others for assistance with these blockages. Through amends and amended living, we actively participate in letting go of the old and inviting in the new. Then we can use the experimentation and effort of Step Nine to fuel deeper exploration and greater release. We seek to be remade, not merely to overcome behaviors.

One closing thought is useful at this moment. As much as

we speak of a different kind of amends-making, we understand there will always be wrongs that must be righted directly at the behavioral level. This can include asking for forgiveness, financial restitution, legal remedies and any number of approaches. As we'll see in Step Ten, there is a place for such actions. However, our larger and progressive desire is to prevent behavioral or attitudinal problems by addressing the root causes from which they take form.

Into Action with Steps Eight and Nine

In your journal, consider the following questions regarding Steps Eight and Nine. Consider first your understanding of your old ideas and decisions based on self by returning to what you've written for Steps Six and Seven. These are the things you'll need to let go of to realize your best self.

Now, how might living amends work? What actions could you take that could become a continuing practice for making amends? Next, imagine who you would be if you were living an amended life, being the person who is no longer ruled by old ideas and decisions based on self. What would you do? Who would you be? Consider this a visioning exercise.

What assets and strengths would you bring to this Amended Self and Amended Life? Or what do you imagine would be developed within you to support this person who has been remade by the Twelve Steps and Progressive Power?

Now close your eyes and imagine yourself in a setting where you are living that Amended Life. Slowly breathe as you scan your body. What feelings do you find? What does it feel like to be that person living that new life? Can you remember any time in your life where those feelings were present? Describe the feelings and occasions where you felt them. Don't rush this meditation. See if you can fully experience those feelings.

Awareness

Step Ten
Continued to take personal inventory, and
when we were wrong, promptly admitted it.

Step Eleven
Sought through prayer and meditation to
improve our conscious contact with God *as we
understood God*, praying only for knowledge of
God's will for us and the power to carry that out.

❧

*"We have entered the world of the Spirit. Our next
function is to grow in understanding and effectiveness."*
—ALCOHOLICS ANONYMOUS

❧

Based on the quote above, it is not surprising that a Progressive Step Ten looks beyond its more common practice. Once again, we do not intend our thoughts to in any way minimize the value of how Step Ten is practiced, for it is a powerful step. Typically, though, we have found several limitations to advancing our practice.

The first problem with our typical use of Step Ten is the tendency to see this step as merely monitoring and repairing bad behavior. It is common in many recovery rooms for people to assume the purpose of this Step is to correct our mistakes. While that is absolutely a fine place to begin, we see a much broader application.

Another problem is the tendency to consider Step Ten to be an action taken as directed by the Big Book before we retire in the evening and upon awakening in the morning. We certainly support those practices, but as the quote above proposes, there is much more practice and value in Step Ten.

Let's begin by acknowledging a potent connection between Step Ten and Step Eleven. If Step Ten is a monitoring step, Step Eleven is a breakthrough tool. Step Ten keeps clean the blockages to Progressive Power, while Step Eleven actively seeks out the flow of the Progressive Power. In tandem they are remarkably powerful.

Our experience seeks to broaden Step Ten to an awareness practice, to utilize it to "grow in understanding and effectiveness." To do that we must learn to use a Step Ten approach in an ongoing fashion, which allows us to increase our awareness of ourselves and our old ideas. With awareness we have the opportunity to avoid acting in ways that prove to cause problems.

Let's take the Big Book language and expand upon it. First, let's note that it does propose the application of Step Ten "should continue for our lifetime." And how might we do that? "Continue to watch for selfishness, dishonesty, resentment, and fear. When these crop up, we ask God at once to remove them. We discuss them with someone immediately and make amends quickly if we have harmed anyone. Then we resolutely turn our thoughts to someone we can help."

Here we see a compression of the principles in Steps Four through Nine. However, we would propose that the focus be more rigorous. Indeed, we continue to watch for the old ideas and decisions based on self that we've identified in our inventory, sought relief from in Step Seven, and practiced amending in Step Nine. With this approach, we create the possibility and consistency of steady monitoring, and, when coupled with Step Eleven, we actively engage in connecting to Progressive Power, which transforms us.

Again returning to Jennifer's story, she can continue to watch for any suggestion within or outside her that men are unavailable, or that she is unlovable, or that she must do something to hold a man's attention. Each time she catches it, she can focus the wisdom of the Steps and of Progressive Power on the solution.

The beauty of this approach is that as our observational and spiritual muscles strengthen, when we are able to see the idea or the urge rise, we can address it long before it causes any action that is harmful to someone else or ourselves. Step Ten becomes a monitoring and prevention approach rather than a repair step. The closer our attention and efforts are to the causes and conditions, the greater the possibility of remedy and resolution.

It is worth noting that initially the intensity of the approach can exhaust us. Partly this is because paying careful attention demands a great deal of energy. Furthermore, we find that our old ideas are invariably operating without our knowledge all day long, so there is a great deal of inventory material. But over time our energy grows because the channel within us stays clearer and our skills and capacity grow as we feel the flow of Progressive Power.

One result of this is that we create a positive, upward spiraling in our recovery practices. Of course! Our Step Ten work becomes progressively effective, and we grow progressively.

Now, when we experience the clarity from meditation via Step Eleven, we see there is an immense upside. We are able to construct a monitoring, channel-clearing and Progressive Power-seeking mechanism that is nothing short of miraculous.

Better still, it is our experience that there can be amazing movement in the underlying causes and conditions that are the foundation of not just our alcoholism, or addiction, but of our life challenges.

There is a notion in Step Six in the *Twelve Steps and Twelve Traditions* that applies. It is this kind of inner work, demanding though it may seem, that determines the difference between the adults and the children. It asks a lot of us to practice Step Ten at this depth, and yet it is a means to unleash a Progressive Power that pours through us.

A Toolkit for a Progressive Step Ten

Of all the Steps, we find that a progressive approach to Step Ten almost immediately yields results. There is simply no substitute for an ongoing application of the approach. As a result, we have some suggestions that facilitate that practice.

- The power of capturing our Step Ten work on an ongoing basis is huge. In addition to your journal, we encourage you to use any extra tools that would help—a pocket notepad, a voice recording tool, an app for your electronic devices. Don't let someone else's preference or prejudice in favor of writing with pen and paper keep you from using your cell phone, tablet or computer if you find that works better for you.

- Similarly, we find that regular dialogue with another human being can vastly enhance our work. Some have trusted friends on speed dial, or available by text message, or using voicemail. There is something powerful about admitting something to another human being. We think in part this must be because the onus is on us to understand things well enough to explain to someone, and perhaps to hear things from them that uncover our already existing but unconscious wisdom.

- There are a number of useful books that facilitate awareness including *Awareness: Conversations with the Masters* by Anthony de Mello, *One Breath at a Time* by Kevin Griffin and Eckhart Tolle's *The Power of Now*.

- Again, we find therapy to be a powerful tool in this arena. And in some cases, personality assessments can help us better see ourselves.

Into Action with Step Ten and Step Eleven in Tandem

In your journal, consider the following questions regarding the continuous use of Steps Ten and Eleven. Consider first your understanding of your old ideas and decisions based on self by returning to what you've written for Step Six and Seven. Then return to your writings around living amends or living the amended life in Steps Eight and Nine. These set the scene for active monitoring work. Next, decide how you will keep track of these things: a journal or notepad, cell phone notes, or pocket recorder will suffice.

Begin by writing down what you'll be continuing to watch for. For example, the tip of the iceberg are behaviors such as anger, acting badly or punishing others or ourselves, or silence or withdrawal. Beneath the surface might be a feeling of having been injured, or resentment, or harsh self-critique. Further down we may see the actual emotions arising as butterflies in our gut, tension in the neck, or twitching fingers or legs. Still further down might be a sense of foreboding, fear or even triumph. Beneath these we invariably find the causes and conditions, the beliefs, perceptions, and expectations that point toward old ideas and decisions based on self. Our goal is to be aware and ideally to become aware long before we see behavior or symptoms, then to try to connect the dots to the underlying challenges. Before proceeding, write down such indicators that you'll want to monitor.

Next, see if you can do something comparable for your assets or strengths. While the tendency in recovery is to focus only on our failings, it is dishonest to overlook signs of our progress and successes, to say nothing of the strengths we all have. Invariably we find we really are good people with ample good intent. Write down the indicators you'd like to monitor. Don't be shy. It is not self-centered to state the positive truths about ourselves.

How will you use prayer or meditation and weave them into Step Ten practices? Be specific. It is easier to remain committed when you are clear on the commitments you make for yourself.

Here are some questions we have found to be helpful when using Step Ten as a monitoring practice:

- In observing this item, is it possible to link it to other parts of my inventory? Are they related?
- Are there particular feelings in the body that are part of the pattern? Are the feelings familiar, i.e., have they occurred at other times? If so, what were the circumstances and how could that be related?
- Do you see judgments or strongly held opinions about yourself or others?
- Can you see how strengths or assets can be involved or related to challenges?
- What would you have to let go of to experience relief, or a breakthrough?

Note: It only matters that you are monitoring. Whether you observe a problematic or beneficial behavior, or whether it is an underlying expectation of yourself or others, or even a core belief that is part of who you are, there is nothing that is wrong to monitor. Ultimately it is the monitoring which produces the awareness we desire. Sometimes it seems that Progressive Power is just waiting for us to make ourselves available for transformation, and acts upon and through us when we are finally ready.

The Twelfth Step and Beyond

Step Twelve

Having had a spiritual awakening as a result of these steps, we tried to carry this message to other alcoholics, and to practice these principles in all our affairs.

Thriving

*Our deepest fear is not that we are inadequate.
Our deepest fear is that we are powerful beyond
measure. It is our light not our darkness that most
frightens us. We ask ourselves, who am I to be brilliant,
gorgeous, talented and fabulous? Actually, who are you
not to be? You are a child of God. Your playing small
does not serve the world. There's nothing enlightened
about shrinking so that other people won't feel insecure
around you. We were born to make manifest the glory of
God that is within us. It's not just in some of us; it's in
everyone. And as we let our own light shine, we
unconsciously give other people permission to do the
same. As we are liberated from our own fear,
our presence liberates others.*

—MARIANNE WILLIAMSON

In the early parts of our recovery, there is a great emphasis placed upon service to others as an expression of Step Twelve. In part, this is because of the depths of self-centeredness with which many of us are enmeshed. And not just as a demanding alcoholic or addict, but often as a more gracious type, a people-pleaser. It is thought that in focusing beyond ourselves, we will be able to break free from self-absorption.

And yet, through working the Twelve Steps, it becomes clear that even when we turn our attention to others, to service, or to the message, we cannot not make things to be about us. Our only frame of reference is ourselves, just like all other humans.

Still, there is value in keeping an alcoholic or addict focused beyond themselves. At a minimum, it will keep us from dwelling on our pains and sorrows. It will keep us busy, which is much better than drinking or drugging. In addition, that outward effort will give us a sense of usefulness. For the newly recovering person now facing the carnage of their lives and doing so without the relief of a drink or a drug, seeing something useful about ourselves is a powerful tonic and motivator.

However, many of us find that there is danger in what some call the "AA Two-Step," admitting we are powerless over alcohol via Step One, then immediately jumping to focusing on others as an expression of Step Twelve. It avoids the critical part of inner work and housecleaning that makes enduring sobriety possible. "Trust in God, clean house, and work with others" does not work very well over time when the middle element is omitted. It is Steps Two through Eleven that clear away the blockages to Progressive Power that will restore us to wholeness.

There is certainly no harm in this outward focus, as long as it does not encourage what some call "spiritual bypassing." In other words, avoiding the challenging inner work of the

Steps for the temporary high of service work or working with others.

You can't give away what you don't have. And it is the inner work of the entirety of the Steps that provides the message and the sobriety that is to be delivered to others.

Now let's look again to Step Twelve. Everything after the first clause is conditional. Having had a spiritual awakening as a result of these Steps ... sets the scene for all that is to come. Calling back to Step Two, what awaits us is a progressive restoration of sanity, which becomes a progressive realization of the benefits of recovery and sobriety.

Those of us who are in a long-term Progressive Recovery will tell you that we needed to reset our expectations; we needed an upgrade. Thriving is the intended outcome of the Twelve Steps. Flourishing. Blossoming. Being returned to wholeness we cannot recall. It turns out that the Big Book notion of "happy, joyous and free" is likewise progressive.

This is an important idea. As long as our old idea is that we are broken, tragic, failed human beings, the old ideas hold us back from realization of our human, worldly and spiritual potential.

Lest you fear that somehow this will simply become a self-serving approach, if we work our program of recovery progressively over time, we should not fear that self-centeredness or the disease of alcoholism or addiction will prevent us from thriving, or from carrying the message, or from working with others. In all honesty, we don't even need to worry about "working" Step Twelve, because it will "work" us. In the end it cannot be otherwise when the Steps are practiced at depth and over time.

As our inner blockages are addressed and the old ideas and decisions based on self lose their effect upon us, there is a natural progression that necessarily emerges. First, we work upon ourselves. In that process we work upon our relationship to Progressive Power which improves as we progress. Sooner or later the fruit must pour forth to others and beyond through our recovery. Eventually we work the steps for the sake of the steps because the principles within them take up residence within us. They become us. At that point people in need of recovery, in recovery and in the world beyond somehow find us.

And the message we carry should progress over time. Of course! How could it not be? In fact, if our message is not progressing it may indicate a need to work more deeply within ourselves. We are designed by Life itself to learn, grow and thrive. It is the nature of things. It is this that the Twelve Promises point us toward, though even our understanding of these is necessarily limited by the state of our old ideas even as a progressive practice alters them over time.

What would you be like and what would your life be if the following promises from the Big Book were realized to the greatest possible potential? As a reminder, this new idea may frighten us. If you find yourself flinching or retreating as you contemplate these bright new possibilities, please return to the quote at the beginning of this chapter by Marianne Williamson. It is this incredible restoration which frightens us most.

1. If we are painstaking about this phase of our development, we will be amazed before we are halfway through.
2. We are going to know a new freedom and a new happiness.
3. We will not regret the past nor wish to shut the door on it.
4. We will comprehend the word serenity, and we will know peace.
5. No matter how far down the scale we have gone, we will see how our experience can benefit others.
6. That feeling of uselessness and self-pity will disappear.
7. We will lose interest in selfish things and gain interest in our fellows.
8. Self-seeking will slip away.
9. Our whole attitude and outlook upon life will change.
10. Fear of people and of economic insecurity will leave us.
11. We will intuitively know how to handle situations which used to baffle us.
12. We will suddenly realize that God is doing for us what we could not do for ourselves.

It is important now to puncture our own ego. As the last promise points out, we cannot claim credit. Instead we become observers to Progressive Power pouring through us as thoughts, words, actions and being. We become a conduit or a vessel. At best we become midwives who merely bear witness to a magic we cannot create, and perhaps we cannot even understand.

The Twelve Steps take us to a different level of mind,
a mind no longer seeking control, and learning instead
how to live with justice, compassion, curiosity, awe,
wonder, serenity, and humility in a world beyond
our control.

—RAMI SHAPIRO

Here is the best part of all. There is no evidence that the potential for us is limited. Of course, how could Progressive Power be limited in its ability to restore us or to limit its demonstration through us?

This is the reality of the removal of the blockages to Progressive Power that are within us. The only thing limiting the possibilities is our willingness and ability to work more deeply and progressively over time on the barriers within us.

My Blossoming in Progressive Recovery

Tim, a friend in recovery, said, "When I was a kid, there were always cops and ambulances at my house. That was my normal, and it kept happening when I was an adult with untreated alcoholism. I didn't know there was another reality because I'd never experienced it. Then I got sober. No cops. No emergency medical technicians. No jail time. I was just sure that was what it meant to be happy, joyous and free."

Of course, a life free from terrible destruction and disruption is a giant step forward, representing huge progress to anyone who was formerly on some doom curve. And of course, with no other experience it would seem like an incredible realization. Yet a few months or years later, one realizes that one's starting point was terribly dysfunctional, and the progress formerly seen as exceptional is in fact nothing but a small, small step.

This is similarly true for anyone living what most would see as a conventional, contemporary life. Once one has attained some kind of career or livelihood, secured an enduring relationship perhaps with children, and managed to settle into a living space and community, what else is there to desire? Except of course that for most of us, any number of deficiencies begin to appear. Somehow there is always some proverbially greener grass to experience.

Once we attain some degree of apparent progress or success, we believe we have arrived while simultaneously planting the next degree of disenchantment. This too seems to be woven into the fabric of life. Yet until we actually experience a new state of being, we cannot know it exists.

With that in mind, let me share more of my experience, strength and hope based on how I now see the possibilities. For these purposes, I'm really going to stretch this point of view. But before I do, let me explain why this stretching is so important.

If we cannot conceive of a degree of well-being-ness beyond our understanding, it is exceedingly easy to rest on our laurels. Of course, it doesn't feel like we have come to a halt in our growth and development. What we can see is how far we have come from our starting point. So we have the notion that we have arrived. With that can come an inability or unwillingness to grow further still.

It can be useful to imagine the possibilities. Otherwise

we may risk underachieving our potential. Worse still, that which we can contribute to the world may likewise be under-realized. So now we see that not only is it possible for the downward drag of life to cause us to suffer, it is also possible to fail to realize our possibilities. While we can never know what Higher Power may have in store for any of us, or whether we have realized it, we would not want to miss an opportunity for greater growth and development.

With that in mind, it was on an otherwise ordinary day that I found myself practicing meditation with my journal by my side. As best I can recall, it was sometime after my 10-year transition in recovery as my spiritual work deepened substantially.

I remember sitting and breathing with my back supported by the bed. The inner quiet grew and grew. Then seemingly from nowhere, a vision surged forth. I saw myself sitting on the curb in front of my childhood home. I was watching ants come and go. There was nothing I needed to do. All was well. And I was whole. Today I refer to this as remembering myself before my own personal fall from grace, which provided a new possibility as well as an experiential point of reference that I had forgotten.

Whole. What does that mean? I guess to understand it we have to begin by describing the process of inner healing and growth.

When I arrived at the rooms of recovery, all I knew was I felt broken and wounded. I believed there was something profoundly wrong with me, else why would I feel such devastation? There was some strange sense that I had a need to improve myself, to move from bad to good. Then I was told that I was sick, sick with the disease of alcoholism, and I needed to get well.

Those notions were very effective for some time, right up until the moment that a spiritual teacher proposed that in fact I suffered from a spiritual malady. I was profoundly asleep from a psycho-spiritual point of view and needed to awaken. This is not just true for those in recovery, but for all of humanity. Life itself is mesmerizing, and the only solution is to reawaken to our true nature and our true potential.

With time I came to understand that while we may speak of enlightenment, there may be no ultimate state of being awakened, rather an always unfolding process of awakening; that the Twelve Steps were tools for this continual awakening. Key questions were essential in that process: Who am I really? What am I here to do? What exactly is the point of this life?

I remember realizing that enlightenment must not be a destination but a state of being that is always in renewal and progression. Perhaps this is the "trudging the road of happy destiny" to which the Big Book refers.

In recovery there is a rich dialogue about the many ways we experience our badness, sickness, and asleep-ness." However, there is not much reference to a state of well-being-ness and virtually nothing of wholeness. We are apparently not comfortable thinking of ourselves in terms of being well.

The first understanding came as troubles fell away. Then my life and its affairs simply worked better. Slowly at-ease-ness emerged. And with it came spontaneous pleasures.

At this point an awareness came to me. Healthiness and well-being were not the absence of difficulties or failings. I falsely believed in my own perfectionistic ideals. Instead I came to see that the measure I sought was the ability to maintain reasonable inner balance regardless of external factors.

Then came a period of time that ratcheted awareness upward. I began to see that all the standards to which I aspired were seen through a lens of deficiencies. All I had been able to see were those things that were seemingly missing, and what needed to be done to fill the holes in me and my life.

It became clearer and clearer that I was wrestling with the most fundamental of human challenges, what some have labeled the fall from grace, or the ultimate poverty mindset.

After that it becomes more difficult to describe my experiences to date. How do you define something when your only frame of reference is the set of conditions that need to be overcome? But with still further step work, especially meditation and journaling, that answer became clearer and clearer.

While I am utterly human, and prone to every human failing, the soul of me is without fault or flaw. Deep down inside me, and you, is a fundamental wholeness. Nothing can take it from us except our own misunderstanding, woundedness and delusions. We can fail to see it, but we cannot fail to have it within us. We can stop aspiring to it, and fall into complacency or comfort, but its call to us will not cease, even if we do not heed it.

What the Buddhist's call basic goodness, or

Buddhanature, cannot be taken from me or you. It can only be obscured. Never lost, but perhaps never found. It is this my friend Eric Rainbeau points toward in his book *Basic Sobriety: Shambhala Buddhism and the Twelve Steps*.

It is not of the world, so the world cannot contribute to it, just as the world cannot limit it. It is the very heart of the spiritual experience, which in the end is intensely and necessarily personal to each of us.

We are and always will be innocent.

The path back is made with every step.

STEP TWELVE

Relationships

"If we do not transform our pain, we will always transmit it—to our partner, our spouse, our children, our friends, our coworkers, our 'enemies.' Usually we project it outward and blame someone else for causing our pain."
—FATHER RICHARD ROHR

✦

It is often heard in the rooms of recovery that we should not make any major changes or get into any romantic relationships in the first year of recovery. Of course, most everyone seems to try to ignore this sage advice, often at high cost, which is exactly why it is part of recovery wisdom.

We also often hear that before you start up a romance, first buy a house plant. If you don't kill it, you can graduate to a pet dog or cat. Once you've shown you can be an adequate partner to a dog which will love you unconditionally or a cat that is above your opinion of it, then you might be ready for romance.

This recovery wisdom tells a painful tale. In the book *Twelve Steps and Twelve Traditions*, it's stated that we fail to see "our total inability to form a true partnership with another human being." This sounds so hopeless, especially since so many of us aspire to find a partner.

The real problem seems first to stem from our desire to have someone fill up our emptiness. The second is that many of us have a "broken picker." Because we project our unhealed selves outward, we too often pick the worst possible people for romance. And even for friendship.

Let's begin this exploration of relationship in recovery by addressing one of the old ideas we like to use as justification. We commonly hear ourselves explain that we can learn a lot even if a relationship is dysfunctional. True enough, but if we are committed to growth and development, a relationship is not the only way to learn, and certainly not even necessary for growth. So perhaps we should just be honest with ourselves about why we want another human being to share our lives. And that leads us to a different kind of inventory.

Expectations Inventory

Expectations are on a par with old ideas, and they are often just as obscure or unconscious to us. Expectations appear in three forms: what we expect of the other person, what we expect of ourselves, and what we expect of the relationship. To be clear, and to channel the wisdom of the rooms of recovery, any expectation is a premeditated resentment. Worse still, having expectations is the antithesis of acceptance, which is an ability to allow others, ourselves and our circumstances to stand as valid and sufficient on their own. We might go so far as to say that expectations are akin to conditions, and love is supposed to have no conditions. Our standard needs to be to take things as they are. Also, we need to tell ourselves the truth about our inner motivations.

First then, what do we expect of the other person?

What we think we need or want of them is typically the easiest place to start. To meet our needs, i.e., physical, emotional, financial or sexual. To do things for us like take care of shopping, or household chores. To attend to the necessities of life that we may not want to deal with, such as finances or disciplining children. To entertain us. To take care of us physically when we are ailing.

As if these were not challenging enough, there is a whole greater realm of expectations we may have of others. To meet our emotional, psychological or spiritual needs. To have a family with us, and to raise children. To be available to us. To support us. To have our back.

Beyond that, we may expect someone to be honest. Or caring. Or open-minded. We may think they should have certain character traits.

The first protestation is usually, "But aren't those reasonable expectations?"

Only if they are things that the other person is routinely going to do anyway. But many of our disagreements come from someone being unaware of our interests, or unable or unwilling to address them. Or maybe they simply are not the kind of person who has those attitudes or character traits.

The truth is that expecting something from someone who will not or cannot provide it is the height of insanity.

This usually surfaces a question. "If I can't expect them to meet my needs and wants, why would I be in relationship with them?"

That is the most important question. And we'll come back to it shortly after we explore some of the other arenas of expectations.

Secondly, what do we expect of ourselves in relationship?

Much of what we described above may very well apply to us. And in the same way, we may simply not be able or willing to meet our own expectations. After all, there remains this notion of powerlessness through which we much constantly engage and explore.

Perhaps the most common phrase heard in the rooms of recovery is how we "beat up on ourselves." Given our consistently unrealistic perspectives of ourselves, that is hardly surprising. We routinely let ourselves down. Our failure to meet those self-imposed, old-idea-fueled expectations is the source of a great deal of aggression we inflict upon ourselves. One of the phrases in the rooms that seems to ring truer than true is this, "If someone else treated me as badly as I treat myself, I'd have to kill them." That is the perfect contemplation through which to see our sometimes damaging self-appraisals.

Last, what do we expect from relationship itself?

This is an arena with great mischief in it. This is simply because we expect things that no relationship can provide like security, reliability and comfort. Worse still, we too often expect to be validated through a relationship, or to find value and meaning, or purpose. Sometimes we have unrealistic ideas of how a relationship will somehow fix something about ourselves that only Progressive Power can solve.

All these matters are a breeding ground for disappointment, and of course for resentment. Thankfully we can address these expectations via the same inventory approach we explored in Step Four. In some cases, we will see long-standing relationship patterns come into focus.

Remember the point of the inventory efforts is to see and understand our own internal blockages. Then to use the Steps to bring the power of Higher Power to bear on these otherwise unsolvable challenges, for it is a Progressive Power that can and will solve that which is unsolvable by us.

Let's return now to the question of why I should be in relationship with someone if the whole point of relationship cannot be to have my needs, wants and desires met by another person.

Our only choice is to eliminate all the unrealistic expectations to see what is left. Perhaps companionship is one of the few that will stand.

Or we might take a step toward great and painful honesty. What if the only reason to be with someone is to love them … to provide for them rather than expecting something of them? What if our motivation for relationship were to be nothing more than to benefit another person?

A Toolkit for Relationship in Recovery

Here are a few resources we have found to be useful in healing relationship:

- Melody Beattie—A wide range of materials for dealing with relationship addictions at www.MelodyBeattie.com.
- *Touch and Go the Nature of Intimacy* by Judy Borich— An effective reframing of the nature of relationship.
- *The Five Love Languages: The Secret to Love that Lasts* by

Gary Chapman—An exceptional reframing of the ways through which we practice loving others and ourselves.

- *Gift of Love* by Joel T. Goldsmith and Lorraine Sinkler—A deeply spiritual examination of the nature of relationship that is grounded in Higher Power.
- *Getting the Love You Want: A Guide for Couples* by Harville Hendrix—A powerful toolset for dialogue to heal root causes of relationship challenges.
- Pia Mellody—A wide range of materials for healing codependency and love addiction at www.PiaMellody.com.
- *True Loves: Finding the Soul in Relationships* by Alex T. Quenk—A framework for better understanding how each of us experiences and expresses love.
- *Escape from Intimacy: Untangling the Love Addictions* by Anne Wilson Schaef—An excellent examination of how deep addictive tendencies infiltrate our love relationships.
- Terry Gorski—best known for relapse prevention, proposes we would be wise to find a friend and create a romance from it. The traits of friendship are an ideal foundation for romance.

My Relationship Breakthrough as Progressive Recovery

It was a few years after I remarried in recovery. I was struggling with being a husband and a parent, and was largely focused on what was wrong with my wife and stepdaughters. If asked, I would say I loved them, but the simple truth was things were not going well because I was not fit for relating. I could not get fully into the relationships with them, and I could not get fully out either. I suffered. And I inflicted that suffering on them.

On a day that I will never forget, I was bitching about them once again with my sponsor. Mostly he had listened patiently to months of complaining, but on this day, as I once again launched into a string of fault-finding about my wife, he couldn't fail to push me.

"Do you love her?" he asked.

"What the hell! Of course I love her. She's my wife," I replied with great agitation.

I saw a glint in his eyes. "Well, you know, love means no conditions."

Something began to shift inside me, but I could not yet go there. "But ..." I began.

"No buts allowed. Do you love her?"

"Hell yes, but ..."

"Love means no conditions," he again offered.

I struggled with what to say as tears came to my eyes. "What about my needs?"

Now his voice was gentle. "Loving her has nothing to do with what you want."

The tears came freely then and the dam broke. I suddenly realized that I had no clue about how to love. It was a painful moment of clarity. I heard myself speak. "I don't know how to do that."

He smiled. "That sounds like a real Seventh Step. Guess you have some more work to do."

So began a two-year exploration of what it means to drop all expectations, all needs and wants, all desires. To ask nothing of her.

My wife and I continued to struggle, but slow and steady progress came until one day I heard myself say to my wife, "You can dislike me. You can hate me. You can leave me. You can divorce me. But I will love you regardless."

The inner shift had finally taken hold. What I said was truer than true. And I knew it. When I called my sponsor to tell him of my success, he congratulated me, then he told me I now had to learn to apply it to my stepdaughters.

Again came a great deflation as I realized what I was learning. Love is a principle. It is not limited to any one person. It is the slow and steady process of yielding one's wants, needs, desires and hopes. First in one relationship, then in another. Then to all people, and the world, and life itself.

This is what it means to abandon myself entirely to a Progressive Power as the Big Book proposes. It is as if in letting go I am in fact fully embracing love, which is at the heart of all relationship.

In the end, it brought me home to myself. To love myself as never before. Because you can't love others without first loving yourself. Paradoxically, you can't learn to love yourself without learning to love others.

Then I have to come to love for the sake of love, because love is a principle. As we so often say, though not with this level of understanding, "principles before personalities," especially my own.

On Trauma and Growth

*"We seek not just that within us that is uninjured,
but that which is uninjurable."*
—STEPHEN LEVINE

"Restless, irritable and discontented" is a phrase from the Big Book that is heard with great frequency in the rooms of recovery. It is a point of connection for many alcoholics and addicts, shorthand reference for a common emotional experience. Yet it too is a symptom of our maladies, not a root cause. In fact, it might be reasonably proposed that disturbing emotional states are inevitable as long as we walk through our lives driven unconsciously by old ideas and decisions based on self.

If we are able to recall how we felt as children, it is very likely we will remember what it was like to be at ease with ourselves. Certainly, there were disturbances, but if we watch children carefully it will become clear there is for almost all of us a time before we were so ill at ease. This would suggest that we acquired our restlessness, irritability and discontent somewhere along the way. It would also suggest that a full restoration to sanity would be to remedy those imbalanced emotional experiences. Of course, we are human and seeking to practice and make progress, not to find perfection, but there should be much room for improvement for us.

In Steps Four and Five, we acknowledged that underlying causes and conditions can be related to the presence of traumas in our lives, especially as children or through violence. To be clear, trauma is not necessarily the result of a single horrific experience or even a few, but can be the consequence of many low-intensity, invalidating experiences. For example, if you tell a little girl she is fat and stupid enough times, it can and does produce a traumatic effect. So too if a little boy is told over and over again that he is bad or dirty.

Pia Mellody, who is in recovery on multiple fronts and who cofounded The Meadows, a residential treatment center, proposes something more profound. Her work with her own recovery and with thousands of recovering people would argue that all addiction stems from childhood stressors, specifically the experience of abandonment, betrayal, neglect or abuse. She says that children are born intuitively knowing when they are nurtured and loved. Further, we might then propose that the breakdowns in family and community systems that result in a child feeling unloved are the root cause of what we would label "restless, irritable and discontented."

What of the idea that addiction is something genetic, a predisposition?

Most probably, some element is genetic, something different in how the addict handles substances or experiences in the body. Obviously even this is not a one-size-fits-all proposition since degrees of predisposition are all too real. Yet if we were to take two children both with equivalent circumstances and expose each to either a high-nurturance or a neglectful family and community setting, it is very likely that we will see a pattern—that the child experiencing degrees of abandonment, betrayal, neglect or abuse is more likely to need relief that takes the form of an addiction.

We so often hear those who say they come from normal, loving families and communities. Yet when we look more deeply it is frequently the case that what they experienced as nurturance was in fact deficient. It may be their normal, and they may believe it is functional and healthy, but that can easily be attributed to how each of us bonds, how we normalize and the means by which denial takes hold within us.

This is not to place blame. Our parents, extended families and communities really did provide the best they had to offer. At that same time, we can say it was not sufficient. Rather than heaping blame upon any sources, the Twelve Step approach is to own our own reality. The challenges with addiction and developmental problems are ours and ours alone regardless of the causes. While we may not be responsible for what happened to us, we are fully responsible for its continuing effect on us.

What then of our understanding that alcoholism and addiction are a disease? There is no conflict here either. Whether the disease is innate or acquired, or both, it still meets the definition of a disease. It should also be noted that the disease is not limited to the body. It includes our emotions, psychology and spirituality.

In the past, this disconnect from ourselves has been

labeled shame, or stress, or even toxic stress. For some it is pronounced enough to be diagnosed as Post-Traumatic Stress Disorder or Post-Traumatic Stress Syndrome. There are any number of diagnosable psychological disorders that are parallel.

To keep it simple, let's consider that restlessness, irritability and discontent are not our first nature, and that they are acquired. Furthermore, let's consider they very likely predate when we picked up a drink, or a drug, or a substance, or a process addiction.

One important qualifier is to acknowledge that for many of us addictions saved our lives. Since it was impossible to be with ourselves and our feelings, and in some cases awful settings, we needed relief. Alcohol or other addictions provided that relief. Then the addiction turned on us and began the insidious process of ruling and ruining our lives.

More recently, groundbreaking work has been done on what has been described as adverse childhood experiences, or ACEs.[1] In addition to abandonment, betrayal, neglect and abuse, research shows that poverty, hunger and violence in the environment can and do have deleterious effects on child development. Not only can these lay the foundation for addiction, but also for educational and economic under-performance, mental illness, and chronic disease. So too are the capacities for human relationship undermined.

A common response is to minimize or deny. Often it is asked that if this is true, why isn't everyone a mess?

Here is what we can reasonably conclude. If a child has sufficient nurturance, or resilience that is innate or acquired developmentally, the challenges of being human or being in a deficient environment can be mitigated or offset. Unfortunately, addiction and other family and community systems are not typically well-grounded in providing nurturance or building resilience. It is also true that because of any number of poorly understood factors, one child can have a very different experience in the same setting.

In recent years, a most remarkable observation has been characterized by those who study these matters. Through means not yet well understood, the same conditions that can cause great damage such as Post-Traumatic Stress can be crucibles from which come Post-Traumatic Growth.[5] For some, terrible circumstances are devastating and for others they are the seeds for personal transformation.

So the upside for those in recovery is that the challenges really can become opportunity. This is, in fact, the space in which Progressive Recovery allows for incremental growth and development.

Cling to the thought, that in God's hands, the dark past is the greatest possession you have.

—ALCOHOLICS ANONYMOUS

Without turning this review of trauma and growth into an overwhelming exploration, what conclusions might we draw?

First, that while addiction has a genetic component, the conditions of our upbringing matter a great deal. It is important to see there is a tendency to minimize or deny these latter factors, largely because they represent tender and unhealed parts of ourselves.

Fortunately, somewhere deep in our memories is a feeling

of wholeness that preceded our brokenness, also known as restlessness, irritability and discontent. With some deeper work we will likely see that those conditions preceded active addiction. And with some effective support we can find that the Twelve Steps can be applied to these oldest of old ideas. That said, it is essential to see that much of this deeper work is experiential. Usually, the way these old ideas were formed did not involve our thinking selves because it occurred when we were quite young. So written inventory and discussions with a sponsor, mentor, coach or advisor may not be sufficient. In fact, speaking about them sometimes presents distractions rather than solutions.

Instead we may have to look to the therapeutic realm. And in the spirit of open-mindedness, we will need to explore to find solutions which are effective for us. This could include therapies such as eye movement desensitization and reprocessing (EMDR)[6], neuro-emotional technique (NET)[7], and emotional freedom technique (EFT).[8] Sometimes energy healers can aid in releasing and letting go, for example deep tissue massage, Reiki or breath work. Not surprisingly meditation can be very useful, as are physical practices such as yoga and tai chi. As a final thought, one very practical option is a book, *Unattended Sorrow: Recovering from Loss and Reviving the Heart* by Stephen Levine, which has been instrumental as a practice guide.

To be clear, this is a matter of fact-finding, not fault-finding. It is important to understand that how you experienced your life may not be consistent with apparent facts. Remember, our experience includes our perception, and it is fully valid because it is our experience.

Lastly, it is so important to remember that these struggles have within them the seeds of our transformation. It might just be that the third and seventh steps have far more potential in them that we might ever imagine.

How We Lose ... and Then Find ... Our Way

It was early in the morning when a serendipitous email exchange between a sponsee and sponsor told the story of what happens to us. It involved a daily meditation from Father Richard Rohr[9], who is much involved in the kind of restorative work that Progressive Recovery explores. Here are excerpts from Rohr's material as well as the interaction it produced:

> *... our first experience of life is not merely a visual or audio one ... it is primarily felt in the body ... we know ourselves in the security of those who hold us, skin to skin ... But we all begin to doubt this primal union as the split of a divided world slowly takes over ... we begin to see the fault lines in the world—and the rest of life will be spent trying to put it all back together again.*

Sponsee: "Jeez, did you read Rohr's meditation?"
Sponsor: "Hell yeah! Everyone gets a fall from grace."
Sponsee: "I feel such grief for my self that got separated as a kid."

Rohr: "Hopefully, our parents' early gaze told us we were foundationally beloved. But when we inevitably begin to see ourselves through eyes that compare, judge and dismiss, then we need spirituality to help heal the brokenness of our identity and world."

Sponsor: "Isn't this the heart of the need for a progressive restoration to sanity?"
Sponsee: "You mean like Jesus urging us to become like little children again?"
Sponsor: "Over and over and over again."
Sponsee: "Bam! Keep coming back … to being restored!"
Sponsor: "What are you feeling now?"
Sponsee: "I can't stop crying."

Rohr: "True spirituality is always bringing us back to the original bodily knowing that is unitive experience, which is why you cannot do it all in the head!"

Sponsor: "It's an experience, isn't it?"
Sponsee: "It's so fucking beautiful!"
Sponsor: "So let's keep coming back for it."

STEP TWELVE

Useful Odds and Ends

"We realize we know only a little. God will constantly disclose more to you and to us."
—ALCOHOLICS ANONYMOUS

"I am committed to truth, not consistency."
—MAHATMA GANDHI

Progress (or Practice), Not Perfection.
—RONALD CHAPMAN

૭

First, a few words about what was previously described as spiritual bypassing, which means that one's spirituality is used to avoid dealing with discomfort, painful truths and unresolved challenges—both inner and outer. Bypassing can be seen in Pollyanna attitudes like the currently common phrase, "It's all good." That may be true spiritually, but it can allow us to avoid dealing with negative emotions and hard realities. In another fashion, becoming attached to a self-perception that we have no flaws, or the reverse, that we are fatally flawed, can also allow us to bypass seeing ourselves in a decidedly mixed light. Even meditation can take us away from reality by teaching us to take refuge in discomfort, or in seeking to escape that very same discomfort, rather than engaging it in order to learn from it or overcome it.

It seems that alcoholics and addicts of all types, and even the so-called "normal" people, can and do use most anything to avoid ourselves and the realities in which we are immersed. There can be no significant learning and certainly no breakthroughs as long as we remain in our comfort zone. Discomfort is actually our ally. It tells us something needs our attention. When it dissipates, it communicates to us our success, though it is always a temporary success. There will always be one next learning that will be presented.

The work of Pema Chodron and Mary O'Malley teach us that the magic of our own transformation comes by leaning into the sharp points rather than seeking comfort.

Even though we often hear that recovery is a journey, not a destination, most of us still cling to an old idea that is hopelessly unattainable. That old idea is that we think we will arrive at a point where we will no longer face difficulties. Indeed, some may truly believe the whole purpose of recovery and spirituality is to attain a place of nondisturbance. Let's call that the addict's dream. And isn't that the reason we sought escape into addiction in the first place? To avoid unpleasant feelings and experiences?

Reality is simply not that. To expect to be freed from the terms of life is a fool's errand, and only sets us up for disappointment and further suffering. Instead, we aim for contentment and well-being with life on life's terms. Call this acceptance if you like, or being reconciled to our own realities.

No wonder we speak of this path as a progressive one: progressive effort, steady and enduring progress, and a progressive awakening and restoration.

Because these truths may seem daunting, onerous or harsh, let's remember the upsides of Progressive Recovery. Most importantly, if we do this deeper work, it becomes increasingly likely that we will be sober for good. If we persist, we can be emotionally sober for life. Yes, we aim high because to quote Bill W., "The good is the enemy of the best."

More importantly, the evidence of Progressive Recovery is that we leave behind the bad for the good to be realized. Then we will come to the point where we face choosing between the good and the good. Eventually the process and progress presents an ever upward spiral of better and better. To be clear, this does not free us from the vicissitudes of life, rather it frees us to live fully regardless of the terms life offers. Not just freedom from, but freedom to. And the possibilities do not seem to be limited.

Asked one wise, recovering person, "Shouldn't a spiritual program of recovery first inspire us, then reveal to us the nature of our challenges, then support us in overcoming them?" To which another wise person who had a great deal of emotional sobriety replied, "Over and over again!"

In the spirit of such optimistic thoughts, it is useful to return to the idea of assets or strengths inventory. Remember, the starting psychological state of most who come to recovery is a negative self-perception. At best, we think we are bad actors; at worst we experience self-loathing or self-hatred. Generally speaking, we have a poor self-concept.

It is interesting that the typical recovering person is in fact quite willing to be and do better. Very few of us aspire to downward spiraling paths, though that is where many of us arrived as a jumping-off point. Still, with negative old ideas about ourselves that are too often reinforced by loved ones, friends, and the larger society, to say nothing of it inadvertently happening in the rooms of recovery, it is challenging to get out from under such negative old ideas.

It is the purpose of the Steps, practiced progressively, to address such destructive emotional and psychological underpinnings that reside deep within us. It is likewise the purpose of supportive recovering communities to reinforce new portraits of ourselves, without denying our painful histories. Whenever we can, we should engage in strengths-based self-examination. We are rarely so terrible as our inner critics tell us. It will take a fairly large amount of positive input before these new ideas of self-love gain hold. The remaking of our innermost selves is neither quick nor easy, though it is remarkably rewarding.

Seek out those who would call us up, not call us out. Look for processes that validate what the Buddhists call "basic goodness" that resides within each of us. Seek and search for proof of talents and skills. Rest assured they are there even if we do not know it. As we often hear in the rooms of recovery, "God don't make junk!" Or as my long-time mentor says it, "You cannot not be God's kid."

In light of this, it may be useful to take an idea from

Carl Rogers, the father of modern therapeutic practice. He said that what we seek is unconditional positive regard for others and ourselves. That is a way of seeing that transcends judgment of ourselves and others, while at the same time seeing clearly who each of us is and what we do. There is no denial, but there is unconditionality. Indeed, this seems to be the gold standard for the rooms of recovery. There is a great phrase from Al-Anon that says this so very well in remarks designed for the newcomer: "After a while, you'll discover that though you may not like all of us, you'll love us in a very special way—the same way we already love you."

In order to arrive at such a nonjudgmental state, each of us will have to let go of any number of prejudices and a whole host of old ideas. Quite often we hear key questions that arise about letting go of these, and more broadly, letting go of anything. We've all heard the truism in the rooms of recovery that characterizes this problem. "Everything I let go of has claw marks on it!"

How do we let go?

Steps Six and Seven as we understand them in this book tell much of that story. After all, abandoning anything does not seem to be within the abilities of any of us. It seems to be sacred ground, which as we described it, is often made sacred through our toils, tears and suffering.

Regardless, there does seem to be a way to explain the means of letting go.

First, let's admit it is not possible in the context of the human ego. If the self could fix the self, there would be no need for the Twelve Steps, recovery or Progressive Power greater than ourselves. Indeed, one wise woman in the rooms observed that "the Twelve Steps are given to us to keep the self occupied while Progressive Power works things out."

Let's see if we can get a look at how things actually happen within us.

The world of psychology has given us a "ladder of inference," which means simply that there is a laddering effect to our unconscious selves. Everyone has a set of beliefs and perceptions. They are unique to each of us and some strange mix of who we are and what we have experienced. They may be accurate, or they may be fiction, but they are ours. Everywhere we go, there we are with our old ideas.

As we walk the world, we encounter the world. It matters not whether we think the world is right or wrong, it merely is. When we bump into that world, each of us translates that experience based on our own unique old ideas. Once again, the understanding we think we have may be true, or it may be false, but it is ours. Interestingly enough, someone else can share the exact same worldly encounter and yet have a different interpretation of it based on their old ideas.

As soon as we translate our encounter, each of us experiences feelings as a result of our interpretation, and we act based on those feelings. And this happens unconsciously and instantaneously. To see this more clearly, think of how you react when someone cuts you off in traffic. Most of us have the experience of reacting unconsciously in ways that are entirely at odds with what we believe to be true, for example we may believe in certain virtuous behavior, but we don't even think before we gesture or act angrily or hatefully to the other driver when they cut us off.

Understanding this allows us to see powerlessness in a whole new way. We are not responsible for the first thought, or even the second, or third or fourth. While we will necessarily be held to account for how we do or don't act, to say we are responsible for those actions or inactions is to fail to understand reality.

My long-time mentor said it this way: "Everything we do is perfect for time, place, circumstances, and the old ideas under which we are operating at the time." Truly, we could not do otherwise. In a certain important sense, each of us is innocent, guilty only of ignorance and misunderstanding that leads to unskillful actions or inactions. While we must own our own reality, when we finally see that each of us is doing our very best, it changes the entire approach to recovery.

What does this have to do with how we let go?

What we do not see or do not understand within ourselves cannot be altered. You can know you have a drinking problem, but until the full measure of alcoholism is understood, we do not seem to be able to get sober. That's what the entire front section of the Big Book seeks to establish, an understanding of the disease and its implications. As a young guy said, "When it gets real, I get real ... real fast!"

The Twelve Steps are designed to identify the blockages within us that are the causes and conditions of our malady, then to allow them to be altered or removed. The Twelve Steps worked progressively are intended to work much more deeply and effectively toward relieving the core causes and conditions, i.e., the old ideas and decisions based on self about which we are ignorant or that we misunderstand.

When full light is brought upon these, they fall away as if they are shadows in sunlight. We don't let go because we do not have the power to do so. We are released when causes and conditions are illuminated.

What about being responsible?

We are certainly accountable. No one else can be. Yet to say we are responsible presumes we are sufficiently aware to act or not act based on being sufficiently conscious. The evidence suggests there is much within us and around us of which we are not even aware to say nothing of this matter of powerlessness. Said another young man in recovery from multiple addictions, "I'm not even responsible for the ability or inability to be responsible."

However, if we can find the wherewithal to be worked by the Twelve Steps, and to do so progressively, we grow in what Step Ten calls "understanding and effectiveness," which is to "enter into the realm of the Spirit."

We arrive magically, mysteriously and mystically at sacred ground.

We are reminded by the Big Book: "The age of miracles is still upon us."

STEP TWELVE

Anonymity

"Anonymity is the spiritual foundation of all our traditions, ever reminding us to place principles before personalities."
—ALCOHOLICS ANONYMOUS

"Abandon yourself to God as you understand God."
—ALCOHOLICS ANONYMOUS

Anonymity is finally when you, as you think of you, no longer matters.
—PATRICK K.

Over the years it has become clear that any time one of us puts ourselves outside the conventions of the rooms of recovery and their traditions, we are at risk of being criticized. Sometimes out of well-founded concerns, sometimes out of other matters, sometimes out of rote compliance with the norms of recovery ... always out of fear.

"Do you really think you are so important that AA depends on your anonymity? On the other hand, do you think you are so important that breaking your anonymity is necessary?" This is the wisdom of Charlie B., and it holds the truth in an opposition of ideas, which is the sweetest spot for Twelve Step recovery. There is never a simple formulaic answer where the realm of the spirit is concerned. "Keep it simple," is a mantra often heard, and with good reason given real life complexities, and yet no amount of recitation will negate those complexities.

Long-ago wisdom from Patrick K. is an excellent starting point for a brief discussion. Anonymity has nothing to do with your name, and whether you share it or not. And inasmuch as we must care about the safety of newcomers and others, anonymity is really not about that either. Eventually we have to abandon ourselves. It's not about us. We (as we think of ourselves) don't matter. It is a matter of spiritual principles before personalities. Perhaps then our True Self can emerge, and that really may matter.

In his book, *Broken: My Story of Addiction and Redemption*, William Cope Moyers provides valuable context. He reminds us that at the time AA was established, being an alcoholic or addict was deeply stigmatizing and came with steep costs in the public sphere. Then he challenges us to look at this matter of stigma. The more alcoholism, addiction and recovery are hidden in the shadows, the more do we perpetuate a cycle of shame. That is a toxic factor for recovering people. We have to stop believing we are bad and start living as if we have a chronic disease, or the spiritual malady of which we so often speak. We have to reset the standard for others in the larger culture. It's the only way to break free from the long-standing morality issue. Because as long as we live in the darkness of shame, we inflict incalculable damage on countless others who need to find freedom from their addictions by seeing and knowing there is nothing about which to be ashamed.

There is some incredibly interesting research that shows that we cannot change stigma with information and education. Stigma is changed by contact with those who are stigmatized. We change minds and hearts by allowing others to see us and to experience us. Suddenly we are no longer pariahs, just ordinary women and men who have a particularly problematic reaction to substances.

Each of us may be the only Big Book some people ever experience. Our lives are the testimony of recovery. Not just to those who are in or need recovery, but to the whole social system that contributes to the cycle of addiction.

Getting over ourselves may be the largest contribution we can make. It allows genuine contact with the larger world. It expands our fellowship. It opens the door ever more widely for others.

That said, of course we need always be mindful of our unconscious motivations. Sometimes there is no better way to overcome them than to stumble. That is why we have Steps Ten and Eleven, to learn from actions that do not serve well.

From the highest spiritual vantage, perhaps Joel Goldsmith sees best the idea of principles before personalities. "We become observers of God in action, ascribing nothing to ourselves, not even good motives."

It is for these reasons that I have chosen to break my anonymity; yet to protect, as much as possible, the anonymity of others. If there are mistakes, they are mine and mine alone. I am willing to face criticism because I can no longer hide as if I am broken. For the reasons mentioned above, it would seem to best serve principles rather than this personality of mine.

There is a wonderful line in the Big Book in the sex inventory section. We are told that no one can be the arbiter of our actions or motivations. It must be between us and a Higher Power. This seems to line up nicely with the idea that none of us have any business seeing others through judgment or condemnation. Spiritual recovery is far, far larger than any one of us.

Afterthoughts from the Author

Yesterday's recovery is insufficient for today.
Find a wise path and follow it.

More than 30 years ago, my very first sponsor made an interesting observation. We were in a book study meeting and the topic was on trudging the road of happy destiny, a phrase that many students of the Big Book will recognize. He leaned over and whispered to me to notice how many of those who spoke were using the word "to" rather than "of" in referring to the road.

He was right. Over and over again those who shared inferred that happy destiny awaited them at some future date, some future place, or some future state of being. After the meeting, he shared it very simply, "Happy destiny is right here, right now, happening in the conditions as they are right here and right now."

Little did I know that the seeds for Progressive Recovery were sown that day though it would be many years before the fruit of that idea would be borne.

Recently in working with someone new to the inner work of recovery, it fell upon me with these words:

> It is not uncommon to hear people say that it is the
> journey that matters, not the destination. Wise ones
> suggest that is true because there is no destination.
> We do not arrive ... ever ... and there is no set
> schedule. We continue to grow and develop,
> because change is all there is, though our small
> selves are quite disconcerted by such possibilities.
> In fact, this should be cause for great enthusiasm.
> Imagine being invited to a way of living and life
> that is truly without bounds.

Awakening comes as wave, after wave, after wave. Self-realization is thus an active, dynamic practice. We are never realized, always realizing. That is the truth of Progressive Recovery. It is exactly why Step Ten is characterized much differently than it is often discussed. "We have entered the realm of the Spirit. Our next function is to grow in under-standing and effectiveness."

These are very heady ideas. Let me be very, very honest about the reason for this work and this book.

I am the kind of alcoholic who, left to his own ways, ends up unable to control his bodily functions because of what happens when he drinks. When drunk, I piss on myself, in my bed, and in strange places only discovered later because of blackouts. And in the days of my active alcoholism more than a few people were quite unhappy with the unpleasant effects of my projectile vomiting. On a few occasions, people were surprised that after such events I would very quickly find my way to the next drink. Powerlessness and shame are quite potent.

I come to recovery of necessity. I stay because of the potential and realization that Progressive Recovery offers. A big upside is necessary in order to stay enthused. An ugly bottom is a good motivator.

With that, it is amazing that the whole of recovery boils down to understanding how we are blocked off from power. We don't have to understand the power, and we don't have to find the power. We simply have to deal with what stands in the way of that power flowing. That is the purpose of the Twelve Steps.

When practiced more and more deeply over time, more and more, the power flows. Not my power. Not your power. Just a power greater than ourselves. A Progressive Power.

From my experience strength and hope, and wise conversations with others involved in this Progressive Recovery, there are a few suggestions that are likely to serve us well.

Study of the Steps and principles is incredibly valuable. Not merely talking, or reading, but genuinely exploring the why and how of the mechanisms of recovery. That requires effort which will likely include research, writing, focus and dialogue. And endless rounds of practice. Progress may be our desire, but practice is our reality.

Since the rooms of recovery are a "spiritual kindergarten," exploration beyond the usual bounds can be very fruitful. Any number of people, teachers and masters have information from which we can learn and grow. We may be unique in our addictive response to substances, but we are not at all unusual when it comes to spirituality. While each of us must find our own spiritual path, we are never, and can never, be alone.

Please consider professional assistance. While recovery may have great materials and community, counselors and medical practitioners have much to contribute. And many of us have much to be gained when in their care.

Some of us have decided to create Progressive Recovery groups of one kind or another. Just like the proliferation of AA, NA, Al-Anon, CoDA, and countless others, there is no specific formula. Yet the Twelve Steps and Twelve Traditions are reliable and durable. So too are resentments, which remain the fuel for still more experimentation. Of course, failure is the laboratory for success. We urge you to fail early and fail often.

It is likely that a supplement will follow this book, one that focuses on the stories of progressive recoveries. In the meantime, www.ProgressiveRecovery.org is a free resource where ideas will continue to be furthered, and stories will continue to be told.

No matter what you face, there is no substitute for never quitting quitting. As we so often hear, keep coming back. And don't quit before the miracle happens. This is true of every obstacle we encounter.

Now to close with a quote from much earlier in this book.

In the end, it is my experience, strength and hope that the purpose of the Twelve Steps, practiced progressively, is to restore us to wholeness for the very first time. That restoration happens in stage after stage after stage, seemingly without end. The possibilities and potential are only limited by our ability to practice the work of spiritual recovery just one more time at greater depth.

Ancient ones believed that every human must forget their wholeness early in life. Yet each of us is forgetful in our own unique way. Thus, our rememberment must necessarily be unique and personal to each of us.

"One does not become enlightened by imagining figures of light, but by making the darkness conscious."

—CARL JUNG

Acknowledgements—
With Gratitude

These ideas have been more than 30 years in the making. Much of the credit for that goes to a Progressive Power that I simply cannot fathom. How it is I am not dead from alcoholism, or tobacco smoke, or gambling, or drugs, or relationship addiction is a mystery. What is even more remarkable is that the calling to do this inner work and to create Progressive Recovery is not something for which I can claim any credit. Perhaps in this case my compulsive nature has served well, a demonstration of a so-called character defect bearing fruit in an unexpected way.

Regardless, I am profoundly grateful. Not because I always feel grateful, which is irrelevant though sometimes quite pleasant, but because I can see so clearly how very fortunate I am. As best I can tell, that is not of my doing.

However, it is likewise clear to me that I am deeply indebted to a host of others.

The teachers who have changed me are cause to marvel. Deep thanks to Patricia O'Gorman, Patrick K., Sam D., Joel Goldsmith, Pia Mellody, Tom Selby, Judy Borich, Susan Olson and Hania Stromberg.

To a small cadre of those who have held me up on an

ongoing basis, a deep bow of respect and love to Chris Anderson, Lydia Ashanin, Art Carpenter, Lezlie Davis, LaVerne Ferguson, Patti Fox, Amy Hood, Maggie Neville, Susan Rees, Karen Van Cleve and Roby Wallace.

And a special thanks to so many who have played with me so patiently in this emerging Progressive Recovery space, even though some of you may not have known it: Charlie B., Chanda B., Andy and Marla D., Theresa G., Joni G., Allison G., Casey H., Linda J., Becky P, Michelle P. (aka Emily), Michelle P., Mamie S., Amy S., Debbie M., Janine T., and Nance W.

To Al Cotton, Sarah Thuerk and Eric Rainbeau, exceptional editors and wordsmiths, and teachers of high order, thank you. And were it not for the guidance and support of Monique Inge, Mari Angulo and Lila Romero, this book would never have taken such fine form.

To Natalie and Brianne, my daughters, you may never know how much you have taught me. As they say in the rooms of recovery, sometimes the best I can do is to be a bad example in order to promote learning.

How could it ever be possible without the meeting rooms and all the wise women and men who continue to create that remarkable space. Said Rami Shapiro, "In the rooms there are people really trying to face reality. I love that."

Some years ago, I went to a twelve-step meeting in Denver, Colorado. It was an unusual discussion topic: to tell a story of an unsung moment when someone inexplicably saved your ass. The leader of the discussion told us to set aside the sponsors, and therapists, and loved ones in order to relate the remarkable and often small miracles.

It was an extraordinary meeting, proof that we are the products of hundreds and thousands of small contributions to our lives and recovery. It was very clear we miss most all of them. We just overlook them.

For all those moments that all you unsung heroes and heroines contributed, we are all so deeply and unknowingly indebted.

Said Meister Eckhart, the Christian mystic, "If the only prayer you ever say in your whole life is thank you, it will be enough."

Thank you.

Notes

1. Adverse Childhood Experiences (ACEs) including stressors, trauma and self-assessment: https://www.npr.org/sections/health-shots/2015/03/02/387007941/take-the-ace-quiz-and-learn-what-it-does-and-doesnt-mean

2. Attachment Disorder: https://www.themeadows.com/blog/item/308-attachment-theory-and-the-developmental-consequences-of-relational-trauma-by-dr-jon-caldwell-d-o

3. Michael Pollan, *How to Change Your Mind: What the New Science of Psychedelics Teaches Us About Consciousness, Dying, Addiction, Depression and Transcendence*

4. Dr. Gabor Mate, *In the Realm of Hungry Ghosts*

5. Post-Traumatic Growth: http://www.apa.org/monitor/2016/11/growth-trauma.aspx

6. Eye Movement Desensitization and Reprocessing (EMDR), http://www.emdr.com/what-is-emdr/

7. Neuro Emotional Technique (NET),
   https://www.netmindbody.com/

8. Emotional Freedom Technique (EFT),
   https://eft.mercola.com/

9. Father Richard Rohr,
   http://www.cac.org

Bibliography

Twelve Step Recovery and Related Websites

Adult Children of Alcoholics and Dysfunctional Families—
  AdultChildren.org

Alcoholics Anonymous—AA.org

Al-Anon Family Groups—Al-Anon.org

Co-Dependents Anonymous—coda.org

History of Alcoholics Anonymous—Silkwork.net

The Next Frontier: Emotional Sobriety

AA Resources

Alcoholics Anonymous (the Big Book)

Came to Believe

Twelve Steps and Twelve Traditions

By the Author

A Killer's Grace

*Breathing, Releasing and Breaking Through: A Practice for
  Seeing True* (Audio)

My Name is Wonder: A Tale of Adventure

Seeing True: Ninety Contemplations in Ninety Days
The Way of Spirit (Audio)
What a Wonderful World: Seeing Through New Eyes

Websites

ProgressiveRecovery.org
SeeingTrue.com
RonaldChapman.com

Authors and Books

Al-Anon Family Groups, *Blueprints for Progress*
Borich, Judy, *Touch and Go the Nature of Intimacy*
Chapman, Gary, *The Five Love Languages: The Secret to Love that Lasts*
De Mello, Anthony, *Awareness: Conversations with the Masters*
Goldsmith, Joel S., *The Art of Meditation*
Goldsmith, Joel S. and Lorraine Sinkler, *The Gift of Love*
Griffin, Kevin, *One Breath at a Time: Buddhism and the Twelve Steps*
Hendrix, Harville, *Getting the Love You Want: A Guide for Couples*
Jacobs-Stewart, Therese, *Mindfulness and the 12 Steps*
Levine, Stephen, *Unattended Sorrow*
Liquorman, Wayne, *The Way of Powerlessness*
Moyers, William Cope, *Broken: My Story of Addiction and Redemption*

Mary O'Malley: *What's In The Way Is The Way*

Bill P. and Todd W., *Drop the Rock: Removing Character Defects*

Quenk, Alex T., *True Loves: Finding the Soul in Relationships*

Rainbeau, Eric, *Basic Sobriety: Shambhala Buddhism and the Twelve Steps*

Rath, Tom, *StrengthsFinder 2.0*

Rohr, Richard, *Breathing Under Water: Spirituality and the Twelve Steps*

Schaef, Anne Wilson, *Escape from Intimacy: Untangling the Love Addictions*

Shapiro, Rami, *Recovery-The Sacred Art*

Tolle, Eckhart, *The Power of Now*

Williamson, Marianne, *A Return to Love*

Authors

Beattie, Melody—MelodieBeattie.com

Chodron, Pema—PemaChodronFoundation.org

Gorski, Terry—TGorski.com

Mellody, Pia—PiaMellody.com

O'Gorman, Patricia—OgormanDiaz.org

51429055R00107

Made in the USA
Columbia, SC
17 February 2019